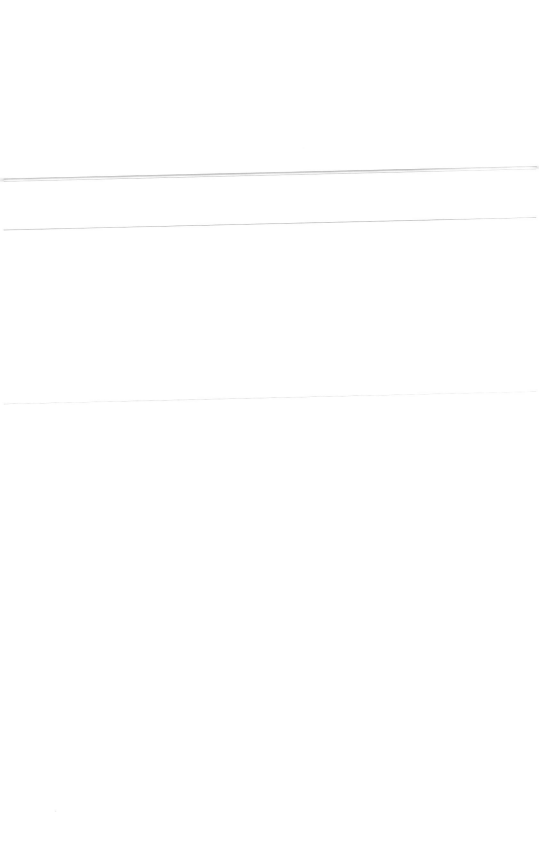

# 1 MONTH OF
# FREE
# READING

at

## www.ForgottenBooks.com

By purchasing this book you are eligible for one month membership to ForgottenBooks.com, giving you unlimited access to our entire collection of over 1,000,000 titles via our web site and mobile apps.

To claim your free month visit: www.forgottenbooks.com/free166186

ISBN 978-0-484-30573-0
PIBN 10166186

# Maryville College
# Bulletin

Vol. XVII    MAY, 1918    No. 1

## CONTENTS

Published four times a year by

### MARYVILLE COLLEGE
Maryville, Tennessee

Entered May 24, 1904, at Maryville, Tenn., as second-class
matter, under Act of Congress of July 16, 1894

A Group of College Buildings

# *Maryville College Bulletin*

## *ANNUAL CATALOG NUMBER*

Register for 1917-1918

Announcements for

1918-1919

The war has involved even the colleges in the unusual and abnormal conditions prevailing generally, and the management, therefore, reserves the right to make changes necessitated by the war without further notice.

*Published by*
*MARYVILLE COLLEGE*
*College Station*
*Maryville, Tennessee*

# THE DIRECTORS

## CLASS OF 1918

Hon. William Leonidas Brown...........................Philadelphia
Rev. Newton Wadsworth Cadwell, D.D.............Atlantic City, N. J.
James Moses Crawford, Esq......................Fountain City, R. D. 1
Rev. John Baxter Creswell, B.A....................................Bearden
Rev. William Robert Dawson, D.D...................South Knoxville
Rev. Calvin Alexander Duncan, D.D......................Harriman
Rev. John Samuel Eakin, B.A...................................Knoxville
Rev. Woodward Edmund Finley, D.D..................Marshall, N. C.
Samuel O'Grady Houston, B.A...............................Knoxville
* Humphrey Gray Hutchison, M.D...........................Vonore
John Riley Lowry, B.S.........................................Knoxville
Colonel John Beaman Minnis...............................Knoxville

## CLASS OF 1919

Rev. John McKnitt Alexander, B.A..........................Maryville
James Addison Anderson, Esq...................Fountain City, R. D. 1
Hon. Thomas Nelson Brown, M.A............................Maryville
Hon. John Calvin Crawford, B.A., LL.B....................Maryville
Judge Jesse Seymour L'Amoreaux...................New York, N. Y.
Rev. Thomas Judson Miles, M.A..................Knoxville, R. D. 10
Fred Lowry Proffitt, B.A......................................Maryville
Rev. John C. Ritter, B.A.......................................Knoxville
Hon. John Powel Smith.......................National Soldiers' Home
Rev. J. Ross Stevenson, D.D., LL.D.....................Princeton, N. J.
James Martin Trimble, Esq...............................Chattanooga
Rev. David Gourley Wylie, D.D., LL.D..............New York, N. Y.

## CLASS OF 1920

Rev. Robert Lucky Bachman, D.D..........................Jonesboro
Rev. Joseph McClellan Broady, D.D.................Birmingham, Ala.
Rev. Henry Seymour Butler, D.D..................Washington, D. C.
Rev. Edgar Alonzo Elmore, D.D..........................Chattanooga
Hon. Moses Houston Gamble, M.A............................Maryville
Rev. Robert Isaacs Gamon, D.D..............................Knoxville
Hon. William Alexander Lyle............................Dandridge
Alexander Russell McBath, Esq............................Knoxville
Hon. William Anderson McTeer............................Maryville
William Edwin Minnis, Esq...............................New Market
Rev. John Grant Newman, D.D.....................Philadelphia, Pa.
Rev. Samuel Tyndale Wilson, D.D..........................Maryville

* Died December 30, 1917.

# COMMITTEES AND OFFICERS

**Officers of the Directors:**

REV. EDGAR ALONZO ELMORE, D.D., *Chairman;* FRED LOWRY PROFFITT, *Recorder and Treasurer.*

**Committees of the Directors:**

*Executive:* HON. WILLIAM ANDERSON MCTEER, *Chairman;* HON. THOMAS NELSON BROWN, *Secretary;* and REV. WILLIAM ROBERT DAWSON, D.D., REV. JOHN MCKNITT ALEXANDER, and HON. MOSES HOUSTON GAMBLE.

*Professors and Teachers:* REV. WILLIAM ROBERT DAWSON, D.D., *Chairman;* DEAN JASPER CONVERSE BARNES, *Secretary;* and HON. WILLIAM ANDERSON MCTEER, HON. THOMAS NELSON BROWN, PRESIDENT SAMUEL TYNDALE WILSON, and TREASURER FRED LOWRY PROFFITT.

*Hospital:* PRESIDENT SAMUEL TYNDALE WILSON, HON. JOHN CALVIN CRAWFORD, REV. JOHN MCKNITT ALEXANDER, and MRS. MARTHA A. LAMAR.

**Synodical Examiners for 1918:**

REV. ROY EWING VALE, D.D., and PROF. CYRUS BRUCE ARMENTROUT, M.A.

**Committees of the Faculty:**

*Entrance:* REGISTRAR GILLINGHAM and PRINCIPAL ELLIS.

*Advanced Standing:* MRS. SIMS, PRESIDENT WILSON, and DEAN BARNES.

*Scholarships:* MISS GILLINGHAM, MISS CALDWELL, PRESIDENT WILSON, REGISTRAR GILLINGHAM, and TREASURER PROFFITT.

*Student Publications and the Lyceum:* PROFESSOR BASSETT.

*Literary Society Programs and Intercollegiate Literary Contests:* PROFESSORS SOUTHWICK and SCHAEFFER, and MISS CALDWELL.

*Religious Activities:* REGISTRAR GILLINGHAM and DR. STEVENSON.

*The Lamar Library:* DEAN BARNES.

*The Loan Library and the Proposed Cooperative Store:* PROFESSOR KNAPP.

*Athletics:* PRESIDENT WILSON, TREASURER PROFFITT, DR. STEVENSON, and MR. BROWN.

*The Cooperative Boarding Club:* TREASURER PROFFITT.

*Care of Buildings and Grounds:* PROFESSORS DAVIS and SCHAEFFER.

*College Extension:* PRINCIPAL ELLIS.

*Recommendations:* DEAN BARNES.

*The Catalog:* REGISTRAR GILLINGHAM.

*Rhodes Scholarship:* DEAN BARNES.

*Auditor for Student Organizations and Activities:* PROFESSOR BASSETT.

*Cooperation with the Government during the War:* REGISTRAR GILLINGHAM.

# FACULTY

## COLLEGE DEPARTMENT

**REV. SAMUEL TYNDALE WILSON, D.D.,**
*President, and Professor of the Spanish Language.*

**\*REV. SAMUEL WARD BOARDMAN, D.D., LL.D.,**
*Emeritus Professor of Mental and Moral Science.*

**JASPER CONVERSE BARNES, Ph.D.,**
*Dean, and Professor of Psychology and Political Science.*

**HENRY JEWELL BASSETT, M.A.,**
*Professor of Latin, and Secretary of the Faculty.*

**REV. CLINTON HANCOCK GILLINGHAM, M.A.,**
*Registrar, Professor of the English Bible, and Head of the Bible Training Department.*

**GEORGE ALAN KNAPP, M.A.,**
*Professor of Mathematics and Physics.*

**EDMUND WAYNE DAVIS, M.A.,**
*Professor of Greek.*

**REV. CHARLES KIMBALL HOYT, D.D.,**
*Professor of the English Language.*

**MRS. JANE BANCROFT SMITH ALEXANDER, M.A.,**
*Professor of English Literature, and French.*

**SUSAN ALLEN GREEN, M.A.,**
*Professor of Biology.*

**FRANK FREDERICK SCHAEFFER, M.A.,**
*Professor of German.*

**†WILLIAM LANGEL JOHNSON, Ph.B.,**
*Associate Professor of Social Science.*

**GEORGE REED SHELTON, B.A.,**
*Associate Professor of Chemistry and Geology.*

---

\* Died August 30, 1917.
† In the United States Army.

*ARTHUR FREDERICK SOUTHWICK, B.S.,
*Associate Professor of Public Speaking and History.*

GEORGE ELLA SIMPSON,
*Instructor in English Bible.*

ROBERT LANDON TAYLOR, *Psychology,*
ELDRED HARRIS GIBBONS, *Chemistry,*
STACEY FRANCIS HOWELL, *Chemistry,*
OSCAR STANTON, *Chemistry,*
*BENJAMIN EDWARD WATKINS, *Chemistry,*
FINIS GASTON COOPER, *Physics,*
ANDREW RICHARDS, *Biology,*
*Student Assistants in the Laboratories.*

---

### PREPARATORY DEPARTMENT

HORACE LEE ELLIS, M.A.,
*Principal, and Professor of Education.*

EDGAR ROY WALKER, B.A.,
*Mathematics and Physics.*

MARY VICTORIA ALEXANDER, M.A.,
*English and Bible.*

ALICE ISABELLA CLEMENS, B.A.,
*English and Bible.*

NELLIE PEARL McCAMPBELL, B.A.,
*Latin.*

*LIEUT. DAVID JOSEPH BRITTAIN, B.A.,
*History.*

ALMIRA ELIZABETH JEWELL, B.A.,
*Mathematics.*

MME. ADÈLE MARIE DENNÉE,
(BREVET SUPÉRIEUR, THE SORBONNE)·
*German and French.*

EDGAR OSBORNE BROWN, B.A.,
*History, and Director of Athletics.*

* In the United States Army.

LENA FRANCES PARDUE, B.A.,
*Latin and English.*

*STANLEY CHARLES LANGE,
*Bookkeeping.*

CARL WALTER BONIFACIUS,
*Bookkeeping.*

GLEN ALFRED LLOYD,
*Mathematics.*

JOEL SAMUEL GEORGES,
*Assistant in Biology.*

DENZIL WILLIAM MOULTON,
*Assistant in Physics.*

---

## OTHER DEPARTMENTS

HELENA MABEL RYLAND, B.A., B.S.,
*Head of the Home Economics Department.*

NAOMI ELIZABETH TRENT,
*Home Economics.*

JAMES VINCENT HOPKINS, B.S.Agr.,
*Agriculture.*

LAURA BELLE HALE,
*Piano and Harmony, and Head of the Department of Music.*

ZANNA STAATER,
*Voice.*

JONNIE WILLIE CATLETT,
*Piano.*

EDITH MAE BROTHERS,
*Piano.*

WINIFRED JOY DECKER,
*Piano.*

---

* In the United States Army.

MARY JANE HARTMAN,
MABEL DOROTHY RICE,
MARY MILES,
*Assistants in Piano.*

CHARLES BENTON TEDFORD,
*Violin, Orchestra, and Band.*

ANNA BELLE SMITH,
*Head of the Department of Art.*

MRS. NITA ECKLES WEST, B.A., B.O.,
*Head of the Department of Expression and Public Speaking.*

HOPE BUXTON,
*Expression.*

* HENRI FRANCES POSTLETHWAITE, R.N.,
*Nurse.*

MAJOR CLINTON HANCOCK GILLINGHAM, 5TH TENN. INF.,
*Commandant.*

MEADE MILTON JOHNSON,
(1ST SERG., CO. G, 5TH TENN. INF.)
*Major Commanding the Battalion.*

HOMER GEORGE WEISBECKER,
*Physical Director.*

---

**OTHER OFFICERS**

REV. WILLIAM PATTON STEVENSON, D.D.,
*College Pastor.*

FRED LOWRY PROFFITT,
*Treasurer.*

MRS. OLGA MARSHALL SIMS,
*Assistant Registrar.*

ALICE ARMITAGE GILLINGHAM,
*Associate Scholarship Secretary.*

* In National Service with the Red Cross.

MARY ELLEN CALDWELL,
*Dean of Women, Matron of Pearsons Hall, and Associate Scholarship Secretary.*

EMMA AGNES JACKSON,
*Matron of Baldwin Hall.*

MRS. CORA HART LOWRY,
*Matron of Ralph Max Lamar Memorial Hospital.*

EDGAR ROY WALKER,
*Proctor of Carnegie Hall.*

EULA ERSKINE McCURRY,
*Proctor of Memorial Hall.*

REV. ARNO MOORE,
*Proctor of the Grounds.*

MRS. LIDA PRYOR SNODGRASS,
*Librarian.*

GEORGE ALAN KNAPP,
*Manager of the Loan Library.*

SARAH FRANCES COULTER,
*Manager of the Cooperative Boarding Club.*

LULA GRAHAM DARBY,
*Assistant Manager of the Cooperative Boarding Club.*

ANNA JOSEPHINE JONES,
*Secretary to the President.*

CELIA ELLEN ROUGH,
*Secretary to the Treasurer.*

* HARRY HENRY FERNTHEIL,
* ERNEST KELLY JAMES,
ANDREW RICHARDS,
*Assistant Librarians.*

HORACE DAWSON,
*Assistant in the Loan Library.*

ERNEST CHALMERS BROWN,
*Janitor.*

* In the United States Army.

# THE COLLEGE DEPARTMENT

## ADMISSION TO THE COLLEGE

Admission to the Freshman Class is by written examination in the subjects given under Statement of Entrance Requirements, or by officially certified statements showing in detail all work for which entrance credit is asked. Admission to the Pre-medical Course requires the same number of units, fifteen, but need not include more than two units of foreign languages. Candidates are expected to be at least sixteen years of age and of good moral character. They should send their credentials to the Committee on Entrance at as early a date as possible. Those that delay filing entrance certificates until the opening of the term will be allowed to enter classes only provisionally, pending a meeting of the Committee on Entrance, and will have no recognized classification until the required certificates are filed. The regular application blank of the College, a copy of which will be mailed by the Registrar upon request, provides for the necessary testimonials of character, a pledge to orderly conduct while a member of the institution, detailed statement of subjects completed, and certificate of honorable dismissal from the school last attended. Entrance credit and classification granted on certificates are conditional, and will be canceled if the student is found to be deficient.

## STATEMENT OF ENTRANCE REQUIREMENTS

The requirements for entrance are stated in units. A unit is the equivalent of five forty-five-minute recitation periods a week during a full academic year, in subjects above the eighth grade of the common school.

For admission to full standing in the Freshman Class fifteen units are required, as specified below:

1. ENGLISH.—Three units required; four may be offered.
    (a) Grammar. A knowledge of technical terminology and syntax.
    (b) Rhetoric and Composition. The ability to write correctly and clearly; a knowledge of the principles of punctuation, capitalization, sentence structure, and paragraphing.
    (c) The College Entrance Requirements in Literature recommended by the Conference on Uniform Entrance Requirements in English. For the texts recommended for study and practice and for reading, see the lists scheduled for the English classes in the Preparatory Department.

2. LANGUAGES OTHER THAN ENGLISH.—Four units required.

LATIN.—Four units may be offered.

    (a) Fundamentals of grammar, and translation.
    (b) Cæsar, Gallic War, Books i-iv. Composition.
    (c) Cicero, six orations. Composition.
    (d) Vergil, Æneid, Books i-vi. Composition, mythology, prosody.

GREEK.—Two units may be offered.

    (a) Elements of grammar, and translation. Xenophon, Anabasis, Book i.
    (b) Xenophon, Anabasis, Books ii-iv; Homer, Iliad, Books i-iii. Composition, mythology, prosody.

GERMAN.—Two units may be offered.

    (a) Pronunciation, grammar, reading, reproduction, and composition.
    (b) Reading of about five hundred pages from simple texts, with reproduction and composition.

FRENCH.—Two units may be offered.

    (a) Pronunciation, grammar, dictation, with the reading of about five hundred pages from simple texts.
    (b) Grammar and composition. Reading of about one thousand pages from texts of intermediate grade.

3. MATHEMATICS.—Three units required; four may be offered.

    (a) Algebra, to radicals.
    (b) Algebra, including radicals, quadratics, zero and infinity, ratio and proportion, progressions, logarithms, series, binomial and exponential theorems, indeterminate coefficients, and equations in general.
    (c) Plane Geometry. Five books, together with original demonstrations.
    (d) Solid Geometry and Plane Trigonometry.

4. NATURAL SCIENCES.—Two units required. Laboratory note books must be submitted to the Committee on Entrance at the time of matriculation as evidence that the student has had sufficient laboratory practice to entitle him to full credit.

5. ELECTIVE.—Three units. Any three units of standard high-school work that may be accepted by the Committee on Entrance.

## ENTRANCE WITH CONDITION

A candidate may be admitted with condition not exceeding one unit, which may be made up in the Preparatory Department and which must be absolved before admission to the Sophomore Class.

## ENTRANCE WITH ADVANCE CREDIT

Admission with credit for college courses or with advanced standing will be granted only upon the presentation of certificates showing that the candidate, having previously had fifteen units of preparatory work, has satisfactorily completed the college studies, or their equivalent, for which credit is asked. Candidates will not be admitted to the graduating class for less than one full year's residence work.

## SPECIAL STUDENTS

The College makes provision for two classes of special students, not matriculated in the regular classes of the College or the Preparatory Department.

IRREGULAR COLLEGIATE STUDENTS.—Candidates offering for entrance a sufficient *number* of units to entitle them to standing in the Freshman Class, but deficient in more than one of the *specified* units required by this institution, may, at the discretion of the Committee on Entrance, be admitted as irregular collegiate students until they have absolved their conditions and attained full standing in a regular college class. Students of collegiate rank desiring to take an irregular or partial course and not seeking a degree may be allowed to select such studies as they show themselves qualified to pursue.

SPECIAL STUDENTS.—Students desiring to study only music, expression, art, or home economics, or seeking only courses in Bible training, are classified under their respective departments. Those whose academic training would entitle them to college classification in literary courses are registered as College Special Students; all others as Preparatory Special Students. They have all the privileges offered to any students, such as the advantages of the libraries, the literary societies, the dormitories, and the boarding club. Young women rooming in the college dormitories and desiring chiefly music, expression, or art, are required to take a sufficient number of literary courses to make up, together with gymnasium and their work in the departments mentioned, sixteen recitation hours a week.

## REQUIREMENTS FOR GRADUATION

The College offers courses of study leading to the degree of Bachelor of Arts. To attain the degree a minimum of thirty-six courses must be completed. A "course" is a study pursued for five one-hour recitation periods a week throughout one term. A term is one-third of the scholastic year, and three courses in any subject constitute, therefore, a year's work in that subject. All courses recite five hours or their equivalent a week. Courses requiring laboratory practice or field-work take additional hours, as indicated in the description of the courses. All college students except Juniors and Seniors are required to take gymnasium work, swimming, or military drill, to the amount of two hours a week, for which credit for one recitation hour is given.

The thirty-six courses required for graduation represent four full years of work, nine courses a year being the minimum amount required of all students. Sixteen hours a week (three courses and gymnasium) is the normal amount of work expected of each student below the Junior year; of Juniors and Seniors, fifteen hours a week. A student is permitted to take four courses a term (twenty-one hours a week) if his average grade in the subjects pursued during the preceding term was not less than ninety per cent. No student is permitted to make more than twelve credits during any one year.

Twenty-seven of the thirty-six courses are required of all candidates for the Bachelor's degree, and are distributed as follows:

English, 6 courses.

Other Languages, 8 courses.

Mathematics, 1 course.

Science, 4 courses.

Philosophy, 1 course.

Psychology and Education, 2 courses.

Bible (English Bible, 3, allied subjects, 2), 5 courses.

Nine additional courses must be elected from the following groups in order to make up the total number of thirty-six required for graduation:

1. Classical.
2. Modern Languages.
3. Science.
4. Mathematics.
5. Education.
6. English Literature and History.
7. Psychology and Philosophy.
8. Social Science.
9. General.

The special requirements for the respective groups are as follows: In the CLASSICAL GROUP, twelve language courses shall be taken, and may be arranged in one of the following combinations: (a) Latin six and Greek (or German or French) six; (b) Latin nine and Greek (or German or French) three; (c) Greek nine and Latin (or German or French) three. In the MODERN LANGUAGES GROUP, twelve courses in modern languages (or eleven, in case Spanish is elected) shall be taken. In the SCIENCE GROUP, besides the four required science courses, seven additional science courses shall be taken and at least two years of German or French. In the MATHE-MATICS and ENGLISH LITERATURE AND HISTORY GROUPS, in addition to the courses required in all groups, seven courses in the respective groups shall be taken. In the EDUCATION and PSYCHOLOGY AND PHILOSOPHY GROUPS, all the courses offered in the respective groups shall be taken. In the SOCIAL

SCIENCE GROUP, eight courses selected from the departments of economics, sociology, and political science shall be taken. In the GENERAL GROUP, the nine elective subjects may be distributed as the student may desire.

## GRADUATION HONORS

The distinction of MAGNA CUM LAUDE is conferred upon such members of the graduating class as shall have had twelve terms (four years) of residence study in the College Department, with an average grade of ninety-five per cent.

The distinction of CUM LAUDE is conferred upon such members of the graduating class as shall have had at least six terms (two years) of residence study in the College Department, with an average grade of ninety per cent.

The Faculty also chooses from among the honor graduates one young man and one young woman to represent the class as orators on Commencement Day.

## CERTIFICATES OF CREDIT

Graduates and undergraduates that have left college in good standing may, if they so desire, receive an official statement of their credits, upon application to the Registrar. No charge is made for this certificate when issued in the form adopted by the College. For the filling out of special blanks, prepayment of one dollar for each blank is required. Duplicates of certificates may be had by paying for the clerical expense involved.

## RECOMMENDATIONS

The College endeavors to help its graduates to secure positions as teachers and seeks to promote those that are now teaching. The records of those graduates that are teaching or desire to teach are kept on file. These records consist of the academic and professional career of candidates, recommendations from the professors or instructors under whom the candidates have done their principal work, and statements from school officials and persons that are qualified to speak of the candidates' character and teaching experience. These records are confidential and under no circumstances are they shown to the candidates. General letters of recommendation are not ordinarily given. Any graduate of the College may register with the Committee on Recommendations, to whom all correspondence on this subject should be addressed.

Superintendents, principals, school officials, and others in need of teachers are invited to report vacancies, stating salary, character of work, and the like, and suitable teachers will be recommended, and their records forwarded for inspection.

No charges are made to either party for the services of the Committee. It is an attempt on the part of the College to aid its graduates in securing positions and to assist school officials in the selection of teachers.

| Freshman Year | Fall | Winter | Spring |
|---|---|---|---|
| English | — | *2 | *3 |
| Mathematics | *2 | 4 | 10 |
| Latin | 1 | 2 | 9 |
| Greek | 1 | 2 | 3 |
| German | 1 | 2 | 3 |
| Chemistry | †1 | †2 | 3, 11 |
| Psychology | 1 | 2 | — |
| History | — | 9 | 10 |
| Education | 1 | 2 | — |
| Bible | ‡1 | 2 | 3 |
| **Sophomore Year** | | | |
| English | *1, 12 | 5, 13 | 6 |
| Mathematics | 8 | 6 | 7 |
| Latin | 3, 11 | 4, 12 | 5 |
| Greek | 4 | 5 | 11 |
| German | 4 | 14 | 9 |
| French | 1 | 2 | 3 |
| Chemistry | 12 | — | — |
| Biology | †1, 3 | †2, 9 | †4, 10 |
| Psychology | — | 3 | — |
| Political Science | 10 | — | — |
| Social Science | 2 | 12 | 13 |
| History | 8 | 1, 7 | 3 |
| Education | 3 | 4 | 5 |
| Bible | ‡4 | 5 | 6 |
| **Junior Year** | | | |
| English | 4 | 11 | — |
| Mathematics | — | 9 | 11 or 12 |
| Latin | 6 | 7 | 8 |
| Greek | 6 | 7 | 8, 9, or 10 |
| German | 5 or 7 | 6 or 15 | 12 or 13, 10 |
| French | 4 | 5 | 6 |
| Chemistry | 4 | 5 | 6 |
| Biology | — | 5 | — |
| Physics | †1 | †2 | 3 |
| Philosophy | *2 | — | — |
| Political Science | — | 1 | 2 |
| Social Science | 14 | 15 | 16 |
| History | 4 | — | — |
| Education | — | — | 6 |
| Bible | ‡7 | 8 | 9 |
| **Senior Year** | | | |
| English | 7 | 8 | 9 |
| Mathematics | — | — | 13 |
| Latin | — | — | 10 |
| Spanish | 1 | 2 | — |
| Hebrew | 1 | 2 | — |
| Geology and Mineralogy | 1 | 2 | 3 |
| Chemistry | 7 | 8 | 9 |
| Psychology | 4 | 6 | 5, 7 or 8 |
| Philosophy | — | ‡3 | ‡4 |
| Political Science | 3, 4, 5, 8 | 6 | 7 |
| Education | — | — | 7, 8, 9 |
| Bible | ‡10 or 11 | — | — |

* Required in all groups leading to a degree.
† Two courses in each of two natural sciences are required.
‡ Required Bible may be taken in any term, but Seniors take Philosophy 3 and 4.

# DEPARTMENTS OF INSTRUCTION

NOTE: The courses in each department are numbered consecutively, beginning with 1. The omission of a number indicates that a course has been discontinued. New courses receive new numbers and are inserted in the Synopsis and in the description of courses in the curriculum year to which they belong. In all departments courses that are starred (*) are offered every year, and the other courses are so alternated as to offer the student a wide range of selection during the four years of his college course.

## BIBLE.
### PROFESSOR GILLINGHAM AND ASSISTANT

* 1. Life of Christ. Freshman year, fall term.
* 2. Pioneers of Palestine. Freshman year, winter term.
* 3. Princes of Palestine. Freshman year, spring term.
* 4. People of Palestine. Sophomore year, fall term.
* 5. The Teachings of Jesus. Sophomore year, winter term.
  6. The Apostolic Church.. Sophomore year, spring term.
  7. A Bird's-eye View of the Bible. Junior year, fall term.
  8. Poets of Palestine. Junior year, winter term.
  9. Prophets of Palestine. Junior year, spring term.
  10. Men and Messages of the Old Testament. Senior year, fall term.
  11. Men and Messages of the New Testament. Senior year, fall term.
These courses are described under The Bible Training Department.

Five courses in Bible and allied subjects are required for graduation. Three of these must be in English Bible, and may be taken during the Freshman, Sophomore, and Junior years in any term. The required work for Seniors consists of the allied subjects, The Grounds of Theistic and Christian Belief (Philosophy 3), and Ethics (Philosophy 4).

## EDUCATION
### DEAN BARNES

1. Elementary Psychology. Identical with Psychology 1. Freshman year, fall term.
2. Psychology Applied to Education. Identical with Psychology 2. Freshman year, winter term.
3. History of Education. A study of the educational systems of early

China, Greece, and Rome; the history of Christian education; the rise of the universities; the Renaissance; and the educators of the sixteenth, seventeenth, eighteenth, and nineteenth centuries. A careful study is made of such modern educators as Rousseau, Pestalozzi, Froebel, Herbart, and Horace Mann. The last part of the course is devoted to the comparison of the school systems of Germany, France, England, and the United States. Text-book, Graves' History of Education. Sophomore year, fall term.

4. Child Psychology. Identical with Psychology 3. Sophomore year, winter term.

5. Problems in Secondary Education. The ideals of education and the problems that confront the secondary teacher are carefully studied. The curriculum, discipline, athletics, social organization, sex pedagogy, and the like, as applied to the high school, and kindred subjects are discussed. Text-book, Johnston's High-school Education, supplemented by Hall's Problems in Education, lectures, and reports by the students. Sophomore year, spring term.

6. Teachers' Course in German. Identical with German 10. Junior year, spring term.—PROFESSOR SCHAEFFER.

7. Teachers' Course in Latin. Identical with Latin 10. Senior year, spring term.—PROFESSOR BASSETT.

8. Educational Psychology. Identical with Psychology 5. Senior year, spring term.

9. History of Mathematics. Identical with Mathematics 13. Senior year, spring term.—PROFESSOR KNAPP.

## ENGLISH LANGUAGE
### PROFESSOR HOYT

*·2, 3. Rhetoric. Punctuation reviewed and persistently applied. Practice in constructive thought as a constant part of the study of rhetorical principles. Reading in periodicals and books that exemplify the best thought and expression, with emphasis upon intelligence that comes from well-founded information. Practice in letter writing and in all forms of narration, description, and exposition upon subjects suited to the student's attainments. Text-book, Genung's Practical Elements of Rhetoric. Required in all groups. Freshman year, winter and spring terms.

* 1. Outlining and Argumentation. Analytical study of the principles of debating applied to the construction of carefully prepared briefs. Method in all composition emphasized. At least fifteen outlines are presented by each student, and criticised and returned by the professor. Five topics, thoroughly studied and outlined by each student, and delivered without notes before the class, are criticised by the instructor for suggestions both to the speaker and to the class. The aim of the course is to develop power in effective public speech. Prerequisites, English 2 and 3. Required in all groups. Sophomore year, fall term.

CARNEGIE HALL.

*12, 13. Public Speaking. The first term's work includes a study of the science of tone production and practice in the delivery of good examples of oral discourse. It involves also some study of the science of effective public speaking, based on a text-book. The second term's work is a continuation of that of the first term. More emphasis is placed on the interpretative aspect of the oral work. During this term a detailed study of the text-book on public speaking is carried on, and the principles are put into practice in the form of original exercises by the students. Sophomore year, fall and winter terms.—ASSOCIATE PROFESSOR SOUTHWICK.

## ENGLISH LITERATURE

### MRS. ALEXANDER

*5, 6. English Literature. A survey of the entire field of English Literature from its beginning to the death of Victoria. The development of the literature from period to period is carefully noted, and the lives, works, and characteristics of the more prominent authors are studied and criticised. Text-books, Long's History of English Literature and Newcomer's Twenty Centuries of Prose and Poetry. Sophomore year, winter and spring terms.

*4. American Literature. Two weeks are devoted to Colonial literature. The rest of the time is given to a careful study of the works of the leading American poets and prose writers of the nineteenth century. Library work and Page's Chief American Poets. Junior year, fall term.

*11. Development of English Poetry. An introductory study of the technic of the art of verse. The forms of English poetry are studied, including the epic, ballad, sonnet, odes, and other lyrics. These forms will be traced in examples from Chaucer to Tennyson. The object of the course is to increase the enjoyment and appreciation of poetry by insight into the methods of the poets and by acquaintance with the best examples of their art. Junior year, winter term.

*7. Nineteenth Century Prose. A study of representative nineteenth-century prose writers, with especial attention to the development of the essay and of prose fiction. The work is based on typical essays of Lamb, Macaulay, Carlyle, Ruskin, Stevenson, and Arnold; and representative fiction by Jane Austen, Charlotte Bronté, George Eliot, Thackeray, Meredith, and Kipling. Senior year, fall term.

*8. Shakespeare. A chronological study of Shakespeare, noting the development of his poetic art; with introductory lectures on the evolution of the drama, and on the contemporaries of Shakespeare. Text-book, Brooke, Cunliffe, and MacCracken's Shakespeare's Principal Plays. Senior year, winter term.

*9. Nineteenth Century Poets. A study of Wordsworth, Tennyson, and Browning, with introductory lectures, classroom criticism, and papers on assigned subjects. Senior year, spring term.

2

# HISTORY

### ASSOCIATE PROFESSOR SOUTHWICK

9, 10. History of Western Europe. A general course presupposing previous study of the subject in the high school, and dealing with political, economic, social, and religious events from the overthrow of the Roman Empire to the present time. Text-book, Robinson's History of Western Europe, with collateral reading and map work. Freshman year, winter and spring terms.

8. Eighteenth Century European History. Special emphasis is laid upon political and fundamental economic matters, such as the Industrial Revolution, commerce and colonies, the internal reforms of the European states, and the general advance of science. Text-book, Robinson and Beard's The Development of Modern Europe, Volume I. Sophomore year, fall term.

1. Nineteenth Century European History. A study of conditions in Western Europe as they have been developed from the French Revolution. The subjects include the growth of republican ideas in France, the unification of Italy, the establishment of the German Empire, and the revolutionary movements of 1830 and 1848; and special topics for individual study. Sophomore year, winter term.

*7. Roman History and Politics. Identical with Latin 12 and given in English with no language requirement. Sophomore year, winter term.

3. Church History. A general survey of the history of the Church from the first century to the present time, with especial emphasis upon the great leaders and thinkers of the Church. Text-book and library work. Sophomore year, spring term.

*4. American History. This course combines and offers in briefer form the work heretofore given in Courses 4 and 5, and is a study of the development of the United States from the close of the American Revolution to the present time. The course emphasizes those things which have been especially instrumental in the growth of our nation. Text-book, Fish's The Development of American Nationality. Junior year, fall term.

# LANGUAGES

### FRENCH

### MADAME DENNÉE

*1, 2, 3. College Beginning French. Designed for those who enter college without French and are sufficiently well prepared in language study to do rapid work. Fall term, Fraser and Squair's Grammar, easy prose, and conversation. Winter and spring terms, composition, reading of some of the most representative authors: Lamartine, Hugo, De Musset, Merimée, and Molière. Sophomore year, fall, winter, and spring terms.

*4, 5, 6. Advanced French. Conversation. Reading of modern and contemporary authors: Loti, France, Balzac, Hugo, Chateaubriand. Representative works of Racine, Corneille, Molière, Beaumarchais. Collateral reading and themes in French. Lectures, in French, on literature. Textbook, François' Advanced Prose Composition. Junior year, fall, winter, and spring terms.

### GERMAN

#### Professor Schaeffer

* 1, 2, 3. College Beginning German. Designed for students who enter college without German, but who are sufficiently prepared in language study to be able to complete entrance German in one year. The work of the fall term is intended to give the student a mastery of the grammar, easy prose translation, and simple conversation. Text-books, Joynes and Meissner's Grammar and Guerber's Märchen und Erzählungen. During the winter term such texts as von Hillern's Höher als die Kirche and Wells' Drei kleine Lustspiele are read and made the basis of conversation and composition exercises. In the spring term Baumbach's Der Schwiegersohn is read. Drill in grammar, together with work in composition and conversation, based on the texts read, is continued throughout the year. Freshman year, fall, winter, and spring terms.

* 4. Advanced Grammar, Translation, and Composition. A progressive review of grammar is made, using Bernhardt's Composition as a text. Schiller's Wilhelm Tell is read and its dramatic structure studied. Selected passages are committed to memory and original themes are written in German on subjects connected with the plot. Prerequisites, German 1, 2, and 3, or equivalents. Sophomore year, fall term.

* 14. Advanced Grammar, Translation, and Composition. Work in composition and conversation continued. Text-book, Allen's First German Composition. Goethe's Hermann und Dorothea is read. Goethe's life and literary career are made the subject of reference reading and written report. Sophomore year, winter term.

* 9. Lessing's Life and Works. His life and works are studied and his Minna von Barnhelm is read. Written reports and original themes are required. Arnold's Aprilwetter is used for practice in rapid reading and as the basis for conversational practice. Sophomore year, spring term.

5. Schiller's Life and Works. Two of Schiller's dramatic works are translated and studied in the classroom, and a third is read outside of class. Outlines of the plots of two of these plays are presented by the students, in German. Schiller's life and career are carefully studied. Junior year, fall term.

7. Advanced Composition and Conversation. Conducted in German. Translation of representative English prose into the German idiom. Sketches from German history are made the basis of classroom discussion and German themes are presented on various phases of German life and

customs. Prerequisites, German 4, 5, and 6, or equivalents. Junior year, fall term.

6. Goethe's Life and Works. Iphigenie and the First Part of Faust are studied and discussed in the classroom. Goethe's life and literary activities are made the subject of reference reading and written report. Junior year, winter term.

15. German Poetry. A rapid survey of the field of modern German poetry, beginning with Goethe and Schiller, including selections from Uhland, Wieland, Heine, Scheffel, Arndt, Körner, and others. In connection with the texts read in this course, the literary movements of the nineteenth century in Germany are discussed. Junior year, winter term.

12. Modern Drama. Representative plays of such authors as Sudermann, Hauptmann, and Fulda; collateral reading and reports. Junior year, spring term.

13. The Novel. Scheffel's Ekkehard, Sudermann's Frau Sorge, and other novels are read and discussed in class. Collateral reading. In connection with the texts read in this course, the literary movements of the nineteenth century in Germany are discussed. Junior year, spring term.

*10. Teachers' Course. A general review of German grammar, historical and comparative syntax, synonyms, and characteristics of German style. Theories of instruction in modern languages. Prerequisite, one reading course. Identical with Education 6. Junior year, spring term.

### GREEK

#### Professor Davis

*1, 2, 3. College Beginning Greek. Designed only for students sufficiently well prepared in other subjects to enable them to complete the entrance Greek in one year. The work of the fall term purposes to secure a mastery of the principal inflections, a careful study of the principles of syntax, and facility in reading and writing easy sentences in Greek. In the winter term the reading of the Anabasis is begun, continuing through the spring term with a thorough review of Greek grammar and Greek composition. Selections from other authors are brought in for sight translation. Freshman year, fall, winter, and spring terms.

*4. Herodotus and Thucydides. Selections from the works of Herodotus and Thucydides. A careful study of the dialect of Herodotus. Special reading on the rise and development of history as a division of Greek literature. A study of the history of Greek literature is begun, based on Wright's and Jebb's texts, with assigned reading in Mueller and Mahaffy. Sophomore year, fall term.

*5. Lucian. Several of the more important dialogs are read, and the peculiarities of the late Attic style are studied. The study of the history of Greek literature is continued. Sophomore year, winter term.

\* 11. Greek 'Testament. One of the Gospels or the Acts is read in class, Westcott and Hort's text being used, with Thayer's lexicon and Winer's and Robertson's grammars. In connection with the reading of the assigned text, a study is made of the general characteristics of Hellenistic Greek, the literature of this period, and the most important New Testament manuscripts and versions. Sophomore year, spring term.

\* 6. Plato. The Phædo is read for the immortal teachings of Socrates, with the Apology or the Crito for his life and death. Brief outline of pre-Socratic philosophy. A study is made of the philosophic dialog and of Plato's literary style. Sight translation from easy Attic prose. Junior year, fall term.

\* 7. Tragic Poetry. Æschylus' Seven against Thebes or Prometheus Bound, and Sophocles' Œdipus Tyrannus or Antigone are read in alternate years, with one play from Euripides, either Alcestis or Iphigenia in Tauris. The origin and development of tragedy, the Greek theater, and other related topics are discussed in lectures and studied in assigned readings. Junior year, winter term.

8. Comic Poetry. The Frogs of Aristophanes is read in class. The development of comedy and its place in Greek literature and Greek life are studied. One hour a week is given to the study of Greek architecture, based upon a text-book, supplemented by lectures and the examination of drawings and stereographs. Junior year, spring term.

9. Oratory. Selections from Lysias and Demosthenes constitute the basis of a general study of the rise and development of political oratory and of its influence on Greek literature. Frequent written translations are required to develop accuracy and elegance in rendering the polished style of the classical orators. One hour a week is devoted to lectures and discussions on Greek sculpture and painting, Tarbell's History of Greek Art being used as a text. Junior year, spring term.

10. The Odyssey. Designed to be a rapid reading course covering the entire Odyssey, of which the equivalent of about nine books is read in the original and the intervening portions in a translation. Merry's two-volume edition of the Odyssey is used as a classroom text. Homeric geography, politics, religion, home life, and art are studied in connection with the reading of the text. Junior year, spring term,

### HEBREW

#### Professor Gillingham

1, 2. Beginning Hebrew. Grammar and exercises, and reading of easy portions of the Old Testament. The satisfactory completion of both courses will enable candidates for the ministry to secure advanced standing in Hebrew in the theological seminary. Text-books, Harper's Inductive Hebrew Method and Manual, and Elements of Hebrew. Offered every second or third year. Senior year, fall and winter terms,

## LATIN

### Professor Bassett

\* 1. Livy. Book xxi and selections from Book xxii. Thorough study of the historical setting of Livy's narrative. Special emphasis upon the syntax. Sight reading. Freshman year, fall term.

\* 2. De Senectute and De Amicitia. A careful study of De Senectute, followed by a rapid reading of De Amicitia. Special attention to the author's thought and style, and to practice in translation. Sight reading. Freshman year, winter term.

\* 9. Tacitus and Seneca. Tacitus' Agricola and selections from the writings of Seneca. A critical study of the historical setting, structure, and purpose of the Agricola. The characteristics of Silver Latin as illustrated in the style of Tacitus and Seneca receive close attention. Freshman year, spring term.

\* 3. Cicero and Pliny. Selections from the letters of Cicero and Pliny. The letters read are such as illustrate the life, customs, and political history of the times, and the characters of the writers. Sight reading. Prerequisite, one of the preceding courses. Sophomore year, fall term.

\* 4. Horace. Odes and Epodes. Courses 4 and 5 present a general view of the works of the poet Horace. By this time the student has a sufficient knowledge of the grammatical structure of the language to enable him to study the poems of Horace from a literary viewpoint. Special attention to the metrical structure, and thorough drill in scansion. Prerequisites, two of the preceding courses. Sophomore year, winter term.

\* 5. Horace and Juvenal. Selections from the Satires and Epistles of Horace, including the Ars Poetica, and selections from the Satires of Juvenal. Origin and development of Roman satire. A continuation of Course 4. Prerequisite, Latin 4. Sophomore year, spring term.

\* 6. Roman Literature of the Republic. The work of this year consists of a thorough and systematic review of the whole period of Roman literature — its beginnings, development, and decline — with special reference to its connection with Roman history. Courses 6, 7, and 8 should be taken in succession. They presuppose thorough familiarity with Latin syntax, a good working vocabulary, and considerable practice in translation. Readings from representative authors. Lectures by the professor in charge. Reports on assigned portions of the various histories of Latin literature and other reference works. The work of this term is a study of the fragments of early Latin, Plautus, Terence, Lucretius, Catullus, and the prose writers of the age of Cicero. Junior year, fall term.

\* 7. Roman Literature of the Empire (A). The Augustan Age. A continuation of Course 6. Selections from Vergil's Eclogues and Georgics and Books vii to xii of the Æneid, Horace, Ovid, and the Elegiac Poets, and the prose writings of the period. Junior year, winter term.

\* 8. Roman Literature of the Empire (B). Silver Latin, and Post-classical Latin. A continuation of Course 7. Selections from Lucan, Seneca, Martial, Quintilian, Tacitus, Suetonius, Apuleius, and others. Junior year, spring term.

*10. Teachers' Course. Intended to assist those who expect to teach high-school Latin. After a systematic survey of the principles of the language, the class considers the most effective methods of teaching First Latin, Cæsar, Cicero, and Vergil. Lectures, discussions, papers, and collateral reading. Prerequisite, one reading course. Identical with Education 7. Senior year, spring term.

*11. Mythology. Given in English. No language requirement. The work includes a general survey of Græco-Roman Mythology, a study of ancient Roman religious rites and festivals, and a brief outline of Norse, Egyptian, and North American mythology. Stress is laid upon the influence of the Myths on English Literature. Lectures, text-book work, reports on assigned topics, and collateral reading in English Literature. Sophomore year, fall term.

*12. Roman History and Politics. Given in English. No language requirement. A general survey of Roman History from the earliest period until the time of Charlemagne, with special attention to the political development of the Roman State. Text-books, Abbott's Short History of Rome and Abbott's Roman Political Institutions. Identical with History 7. Sophomore year, winter term.

### SPANISH
#### President Wilson

*1, 2. College Beginning Spanish. Grammar, translation, composition, conversation. Beginning with the second lesson, the principal exercises are the translation of English into Spanish and of Spanish into English. Text-books, De Tornos' Combined Spanish Method and a commercial reader, and, in the winter term, Galdos' Marianela and El Si de las Niñas. Senior year, fall and winter terms.

### MATHEMATICS
#### Professor Knapp

*2. Plane Trigonometry. Definitions and fundamental notions; systems of angular measurement; trigonometric formulæ, their derivation and transformation; solutions of equations and of numerical problems. Required in all groups. Students that present Plane Trigonometry for college entrance take Course 4 or 9. Freshman year, fall term.

*4. Plane Analytic Geometry. Rectilinear and polar systems of coordinates; the straight line, circle, parabola, ellipse, and hyperbola; tangents and normals; general equation of the second degree and certain higher plane curves. Prerequisite, Mathematics 2. Either this course or Course 9 required of students that present Plane Trigonometry for college entrance. **Freshman year, winter term.**

\* 10. Plane Surveying. The use and adjustments of instruments, and the methods employed in practical surveying. The work includes chaining, triangulation, leveling, calculating areas and earthwork, establishing grades, dividing land, railway location, laying out curves, mapping, and topographical work. Special attention is given to field-work. Prerequisite, Mathematics 2. Freshman year, spring term.

\* 8. College Algebra. Logarithms; series; permutations, combinations, and probability; determinants and the theory of equations. Sophomore year, fall term.

\* 6, 7. Differential and Integral Calculus. Differentiation of algebraic and transcendental functions, with elementary applications of the calculus, especially in maxima and minima, and in the expansion of functions, the general treatment of curve tracing, asymptotes, inflection, curvature, and singular points; radius of curvature and envelopes. Direct integration of elementary forms, including integration by decomposition of fractions; integration by substitution, by parts, and by the aid of reduction formulæ. Applications particularly in the rectification, quadrature, and cubature of curves. Prerequisite, Mathematics 4. Sophomore year, winter and spring terms.

\* 9. Astronomy. A general survey; definitions; description and use of instruments; earth, moon, sun, planets, aerolites and shooting stars, comets, fixed stars; stellar and planetary evolution. Prerequisite, Mathematics 2. Either this course or Course 4 required of students that present Plane Trigonometry for college entrance. Junior year, winter term.

\* 11. Spherical Trigonometry and Solid Analytic Geometry. The development and transformation of formulæ; solution of spherical triangles with applications in geodesy, navigation, and astronomy. Systems of coordinates in solid analytic geometry; loci; lines, planes, surfaces; general equations of the second degree; ruled surfaces. Prerequisite, Mathematics 4. Junior year, spring term.

12. Differential Equations. Equations of the first and second orders; linear equations; solutions of equations by series; miscellaneous applications. Prerequisites, Mathematics 6 and 7. Junior year, spring term.

13. The History of Mathematics. Mathematical knowledge and methods of primitive races; Egyptians; the Greek schools; the Middle Ages and the Renaissance; mathematics of the seventeenth and eighteenth centuries; recent times; résumé by topics with a study of the methods of teaching elementary mathematics. Identical with Education 9. Senior year, spring term.

## NATURAL SCIENCES
### BIOLOGY
#### Miss Green and Laboratory Assistant

\* 1. General Invertebrate Zoology. Classroom work, accompanied by dissection of typical forms, and field-work. Text-book, Hegner's Zoology, with Pratt's Laboratory Manual. Prerequisite, elementary physiology. Laboratory practice, four hours a week; recitations, three hours. Sophomore year, fall term.

* 2. General Vertebrate Zoology. Classroom work, accompanied by dissection of typical forms, and field-work. Text-book, Hegner's Zoology, with Pratt's Laboratory Manual. Prerequisite, elementary physiology. Laboratory practice, four hours a week; recitations, three hours. Sophomore year, winter term.

* 3. Botany. Life History of Plants from Seed to Flower. Emphasis is laid upon the chief problems involved in the physiology, ecology, and morphology of the seed, the developing plant, and the flower. Text-book, Bergen and Davis' Principles of Botany. Laboratory practice, four hours a week; recitations, three hours. Sophomore year, fall term.

* 4. Botany. Plant Morphology. A rapid morphological survey of the four great plant groups. Text-book, Bergen and Davis' Principles of Botany. Laboratory practice, four hours a week; recitations, three hours. Sophomore year, spring term.

5. Botany. Plant Physiology. A study of the most evident life relations of plants, embracing the fundamental principles of plant physiology. Classroom work, accompanied by experimental work in the laboratory. The work is not confined to any one text-book, but references are given out to various standard text-books on plant physiology. Prerequisite, Biology 3. Laboratory practice, four hours a week; recitations, three hours. Junior year, winter term.

* 9. Advanced Physiology. Classroom work and laboratory experiments, bringing out the fundamental principles of the circulatory and respiratory systems. Especially valuable to students intending to study medicine. Text-book, Brubaker's Physiology, supplemented by reference work and lectures. Prerequisites, elementary physiology, elementary physics, and Biology 2. Laboratory practice, four hours a week; lectures and quizzes, three hours. Sophomore year, winter term.

* 10. Advanced Physiology. Same as Course 9, except that the digestive and nervous systems are studied. Especially valuable as a preliminary to the Psychology courses; to students of Home Economics; and to students preparing for a medical course. Prerequisites, same as for Course 9, with the addition of Chemistry 1 and 2. Laboratory practice, four hours a week; lectures and quizzes, three hours. Sophomore year, spring term.

### CHEMISTRY

ASSOCIATE PROFESSOR SHELTON AND LABORATORY ASSISTANTS

* 1. General Inorganic Chemistry. A beginner's course in modern chemical theory and practice. Suitable experiments are selected, but the requirements of the course center about lectures and quizzes, both oral and written. Text-book, Mellor's Modern Inorganic Chemistry. Laboratory

practice, four hours a week; lectures and quizzes, three hours. Freshman year, fall term.

* 2. General Inorganic Chemistry. A continuation of Course 1 during the first half of the winter term. Second half of the winter term, an introduction to Qualitative Chemical Analysis. The work of the latter half of the term has to do more particularly with the metals. The order of their presentation for discussion and laboratory study follows the analytical order as outlined in Gooch and Browning's Outlines of Qualitative Chemical Analysis. Continual reference is made to Mellor's Modern Inorganic Chemistry. Laboratory practice, six hours a week; lectures and quizzes, two hours. Freshman year, winter term.

* 3. General Inorganic Chemistry and Qualitative Analysis. A continuation of Course 2. This is more particularly a course in metallurgical and applied chemistry with respect to the lectures, and in analytical chemistry with respect to the laboratory. Text-book, same as in Course 2. Laboratory practice, six hours a week; lectures and quizzes, two hours. Freshman year, spring term.

* 11. Elementary Organic and Household Chemistry. Designed primarily for students in Home Economics. Laboratory practice, six hours a week; lectures, two hours. Prerequisites, Chemistry 1 and 2. Freshman year, spring term.

12. Advanced Household Chemistry. A course dealing with elementary biochemistry, chemical sanitation, food analysis, and poisons. This is a laboratory course of eight laboratory hours and one lecture a week. Much use is made of the library. The study is topical. Prerequisites, Chemistry 1, 2, and 11. Sophomore year, fall term.

4. Quantitative Chemical Analysis. A laboratory course of eight hours a week in the volumetric and gravimetric methods ordinarily employed in quantitative chemical analysis. The instruction is individual, and there is continual reference to the well-stocked reference library and to current literature. Independence of thought is the aim, and the most scrupulous care to exactness of technic is required. One hour a week in addition is devoted to quizzes and informal discussions. Prerequisites, Chemistry 1, 2, and 3. Junior year, fall term.

5. Quantitative Chemical Analysis. A continuation of Course 4. Junior year, winter term.

6. Quantitative Chemical Analysis. A continuation of Course 5. Junior year, spring term.

7. General Organic Chemistry. Text-book, Perkin and Kipping's Organic Chemistry. Laboratory practice, eight hours a week; lecture or quiz, one hour. Senior year, fall term.

8. General Organic Chemistry. A continuation of Course 7. Senior year, winter term.

9. General Organic Chemistry. A continuation of Course 8, with

some definite applications to biological chemistry, both analytical and theoretical. Senior year, spring term.

For acceptable substitutes for Chemistry courses in the Science Group, see Geology and Mineralogy.

### GEOLOGY AND MINERALOGY
#### ASSOCIATE PROFESSOR SHELTON

* 1. Mineralogy. A laboratory course of eight hours a week, accompanied by one hour lecture a week. Manual, Brush-Penfield's Determinative Mineralogy. Prerequisites, Chemistry 1, 2, and 3. Senior year, fall term.

* 2. General Geology. Dynamic and Structural. Text-book, Chamberlain and Salesbury's College Geology. Prerequisites, Chemistry 1, 2, and 3. Senior year, winter term.

3. General Geology. Historical. A continuation of Course 2. Much use is made of the United States Geological Folios and Atlas. Also occasional field trips are made to interesting localities in the county. Senior year, spring term.

Geology 1, 2, and 3 may be substituted for Chemistry 7, 8, and 9 by students electing the Science Group.

### PHYSICS
#### PROFESSOR KNAPP AND LABORATORY ASSISTANT

* 1. Mechanics and Sound. Lectures, recitations, and quantitative experiments. Prerequisite, Mathematics 2. Laboratory practice, four hours a week; recitations, three hours. Junior year, fall term.

* 2. Heat and Light. A continuation of Course 1. Junior year, winter term.

* 3. Electricity and Magnetism. A continuation of Course 2. Junior year, spring term.

### PHILOSOPHY
#### DEAN BARNES AND PROFESSORS GILLINGHAM AND DAVIS

* 2. Logic. Practical exercises and much original work in Induction connected with every-day questions, the aim being to make the study of practical service in such reasoning as will be met by the student in his subsequent experiences in life. Text-book, Hill's Jevons' Logic, in connection with questions and exercises prepared for the class. Required in all groups. Junior year, fall term.—PROFESSOR DAVIS.

* 3. The Grounds of Theistic and Christian Belief. The principal theistic and anti-theistic arguments are reviewed, and then the main historical and philosophical arguments for belief in the Christian religion are considered. Text-books, Mullin's Why is Christianity True? and Fisher's Evidences of Theistic and Christian Belief. Prerequisites, Philosophy 2 and one course in psychology. Required in all groups. Senior year, winter term.—PROFESSOR GILLINGHAM.

*4. Ethics. The leading conceptions of moral theory are approached by the historical method. The student is led to see that moral problems are real problems, which are solved best by reflective thought that is guided by Christian ideals. The various types of ethical theory are discussed. Special emphasis is placed upon the ethics of social organizations: the state, the economic life, and the family. Text-book, Dewey and Tufts, supplemented by the works of Sidgwick, Green, Martineau, and Spencer. Prerequisite, one course in psychology. Required in all groups. Senior year, spring term.—DEAN BARNES.

## POLITICAL SCIENCE

### DEAN BARNES

10. American Government. The form and workings of local, state, and national government in the United States are studied. Discussion of current political events. Text-book, Hart's Actual Government, supplemented by readings in Bryce's American Commonwealth. Sophomore year, fall term.

1. Liberty. A study of the idea of the nation, and of the character and distribution of nationalities; a development of the idea and conception of the state, and a study of its origin, forms, and ends; a history of the formation of the constitutions of the states of Great Britain, the United States, Germany, and France, and of the organization of these states within their respective constitutions, and a study of liberty as guaranteed in their constitutions. Text-book, Burgess' Political Science, Volume I, supplemented by Story's Commentaries, and Thayer's and McClain's Cases, and the works of other authors. Junior year, winter term.

2. Government. A study of the forms of government, the constructions, powers, and duties of the legislative, executive, and judicial departments of the governments of Great Britain, the United States, Germany, and France. Text-book, Burgess' Political Science, Volume II, supplemented by the works of Story, Macy, and other authors. Junior year, spring term.

3. International Law. The elements of international law, with an account of its origin, sources, and historical development. Text-book, Lawrence, supplemented by prescribed readings in the works of Woolsey and Hall, and in Scott's and Snow's Cases. Senior year, fall term.

4. The Process of Legislation and Parliamentary Law. Designed to familiarize students with legislative structure and procedure, national, state, and municipal. Also a study of the structure and procedure of political conventions and similar bodies, and the theory and practice of parliamentary law. Prerequisites, Political Science 1 and 2. Senior year, fall term.

5. Political Parties. A study of the history, organization, and methods of action of political parties in the United States. Growth of the party system; primary and convention systems; permanent party organization;

reform movements; and the value and theory of the party system. Senior year, fall term.

6. Comparative Governments. A comparative study of the governments of Greece, Rome, France, and Germany. Text-book, Ogg's Governments of Europe, supplemented by Lowell's Governments and Parties in Continental Europe. Senior year, winter term.

7. Comparative Governments. A comparative study of the governments of Switzerland, Austria-Hungary, Sweden, Norway, Great Britain, and the United States. Text-books, Ogg and Lowell, supplemented by Taswell-Langmead, Ridges, Low, Goodnow, Cooley, and Story. Senior year, spring term.

8. Constitutional Law. A brief study of the elementary principles of constitutional law exemplified by cases. Text-book, Hall's Constitutional Law, and McClain's and Thayer's Cases are used. Senior year, fall term.

## PSYCHOLOGY
### Dean Barnes and Laboratory Assistant

* 1. Elementary Psychology. Designed for students taking the Teachers' Course. A text-book course, supplemented by lectures and typical experiments. Text-book, Pillsbury's Fundamentals of Psychology. Identical with Education 1. Freshman year, fall term.

* 2. Psychology Applied to Education. The discussion of psychological problems which have reference to education; theory of recapitulation, correlations between mind and body, instinct, memory, imagination, apperception, interest, work, fatigue, motor control, and volition. Text-book, Bolton's Principles of Education, supplemented by lectures. Identical with Education 2. Freshman year, winter term.

* 3. Child Psychology. Problems, methods, and data in the psychological growth of children and youth. This course is developed with special reference to the dynamic conception of the mind, and mental growth as a function of sensori-motor coordination. From this point of view, attention, perception, apperception, interest, habit, and will are discussed. The course is designed to show the application of psychological laws and principles to educational theory and practice. Identical with Education 4. Sophomore year, winter term.

* 4. Advanced General Psychology. A study of the psycho-physical organism by means of the Auzoux models, sensation, habit, attention, perception, memory, imagination, reasoning, emotions, and volition. Typical experiments. Lectures, readings, discussions, and reports. Prerequisite, Psychology 1 or 2. Senior year, fall term.

. 5. Educational Psychology. Psychology applied to teaching and management in the high school and upper grammar grades; a study of the group consciousness and social instincts of adolescents, competition, rivalry, sex, dress, social organization, with special reference to the meaning of these facts in their application in the organization of the school. Identical with Education 8. Prerequisites, Psychology 1, 2, and 3. Senior year, spring term.

6. Social Psychology. A study of group consciousness and social origins. Relation of the psychic life of the group to the group activities. Instruction and discipline of children by the parents and by the group. Comparison of the mental traits of different races and social classes. Psychology of the crowd, the mores, and folkways. Open to Seniors and to Juniors who have had Psychology 1, 2, 3, and 4. Senior year, winter term.

7. Experimental Psychology. This course consists of experiments in acoustics, haptics, optics, reactions, taste, and smell. Text-book, Titchener's Experimental Psychology, supplemented by the works of Külpe, Sanford, Judd, and Myer. Senior year, spring term.

8. Experimental Psychology. A continuation of Course 7. Special emphasis is placed upon the study of the reaction experiment by the use of the Hipp chronoscope. Senior year, spring term.

### SOCIAL SCIENCE

PROFESSOR HOYT AND ASSOCIATE PROFESSOR SOUTHWICK

*2. Practical Sociology. The units of social organization, questions of population, questions of the family, the labor system, social well-being, and the defense of society. Sophomore year, fall term.

*12. City Problems. The first half of this course is devoted to the study of Howe's The Modern City and Its Problems. This book deals in general with the governments and problems of modern cities in England, Germany, and the United States. The second half is a study of Wilcox's Great Cities in America, in which the problems of six great American cities are specifically discussed. Sophomore year, winter term.

*13. Rural Problems. Designed to show the scope of rural sociology, to compare the advantages of country and city, to mark out the nature of the rural problem, to consider such improvements as are conducive to rural community welfare. Text-book, Gillette's Constructive Sociology. Sophomore year, spring term.

14. Economic Principles. An elementary course presenting the fundamental concepts and problems of economics to serve as a general survey of the subject. Text-book, Bullock's Introduction to the Study of Economics. Junior year, fall term.

15, 16. Economic Principles. Designed to provide advanced study in the field of economics. A philosophic study of the economic principles that explain the industrial conditions of modern countries, particularly of the United States. The organization of production, value and exchange, money, international trade, distribution of wealth, labor problems, problems of economic organization, and taxation are the chief questions considered. Text-book, Taussig's Economic Principles. Junior year, winter and spring terms.

# PRE-MEDICAL COURSE

For the benefit of students preparing to study medicine but unable first to complete the full four years' college course leading to a degree, the College provides a special course covering those college studies demanded for entrance to medical schools of Class A standard, as classified by the American Medical Association. The requirements for admission to this course are the same as for admission to the Freshman Class, except that the fifteen units of high-school work presented need not include more than two units of foreign languages.

The course of study may be completed in two years if taken in the order prescribed in the following synopsis. Each fall term course is the equivalent of four semester hours; each winter term course, three hours; and each spring term course, three hours. The first year's work, therefore, provides thirty-four semester hours, and the second year's work, thirty semester hours. This is in addition, of course, to the two semester hours (equivalent) in physical culture required of all students.

**Synopsis of Courses.**—The following is a synopsis of the courses meeting the requirements of the American Medical Association:

FIRST YEAR

| *Fall* | *Winter* | *Spring* |
|---|---|---|
| Bible 4 | English 2 | English 3 |
| German 1 or | German 2 or | German 3 or |
| French 1 | French 2 | French 3 |
| Mathematics 2 or | | |
| Psychology 1 | | |
| Chemistry 1 | Chemistry 2 | Chemistry 3 |

SECOND YEAR

| *Fall* | *Winter* | *Spring* |
|---|---|---|
| Physics 1 | Physics 2 | Physics 3 |
| Organic Chemistry 7 | Biology 9 or | Biology 10 |
| | Psychology 2 or 7 | |
| Biology 1 | Biology 2 | Bible 6 |

These courses are described under Departments of Instruction in the foregoing pages. A student completing the pre-medical course will be certified to to the medical school that he may wish to enter.

# THE TEACHERS' DEPARTMENT

A large percentage of the graduates and undergraduates of Maryville College become teachers. They are found in all sections of the United States; especially in the Southern Appalachian region, and in the Southwest and West, and are employed in elementary schools, high schools, and colleges.

The instructors in the various departments of the College endeavor to conduct their work in such a way as to help train teachers both by the thoroughness of the instruction given in the various branches, and by the object lesson of the methods employed in the classrooms. Competent teachers selected from many colleges and universities bring the best methods of those schools to their work at Maryville. The teachers trained at Maryville rank high in sound scholarship and practical pedagogy.

Besides providing model methods in college management and class-room work, the College maintains a special department for the vocational training of teachers. The courses offered meet the requirements of the State Board of Public Instruction for Tennessee. The teacher's certificate issued by this Board is recognized by reciprocating boards in other States throughout the country. The Education Group in the College Department leads to the Bachelor's degree. In the Teachers' Department a six years' course of study designed to equip prospective teachers thoroughly for their profession is offered.

## PREPARATORY

**Synopsis of Courses.**—The following is a synopsis of the courses in the four preparatory years:

| First Year | Second Year | Third Year | Fourth Year |
|---|---|---|---|
| Mathematics II | Mathematics III | Mathematics IV | Mathematics V |
| English I | English II | English III | or English IV |
| Latin I | Latin II | Lat. III, Ger. I, | Lat. IV, Ger. II, |
| History I | Science I | or French I | or French II |
| | | History III | Science II |
| *Mathematics I | *History II | | Pedagogy I |
| | *Bookkeeping I | | *History IV |

---

* May be taken as an extra study by permission of the Principal of the Preparatory Department.

ANDERSON HALL.

**Pedagogy.**—Fourth Year: I. This course is designed to prepare the teacher to control and teach a school in accordance with sound pedagogical principles and methods. The principles underlying class management and instruction are studied, and the practical problems of organization, discipline, and method are discussed. In the fall term Colvin and Bagley's Human Behavior and McMurry's Method of the Recitation are used as text-books. In the winter term Seeley's School Management and Charter's Teaching the Common Branches are used as text-books. In the spring term the books selected for the Tennessee Teachers' Reading Circle are used. This course is open also to such students in the college classes as may desire special work in these lines.

**Special Courses.**—To accommodate teachers and others who enter College after the Christmas holidays, special courses in history, civics, higher arithmetic, and grammar are offered. Students may also take up any full-year course offered in the curriculum of the preparatory years for which they are prepared. College courses may also be taken by those who have had sufficient preparation.

**Special Double Courses.**—In addition to the regular courses, and the special courses referred to above, special double courses in Beginning Latin and Beginning Algebra are provided, by which a full year's credit in these studies may be secured during the winter and spring terms. The classes recite ten hours each a week, and prepare respectively for Cæsar and Advanced Algebra. For the successful completion of the double course in either Latin or Algebra one unit credit will be given; for any of the other preparatory courses, proportional credit will be allowed.

**Other Courses.**—Detailed descriptions of the courses outlined in the four preparatory years of the Teachers' Department will be found under Description of Courses in the Preparatory Department. These four years correspond closely to the regular courses of the Preparatory Department, and contain sixteen units of academic work. Those completing these four years are admitted to the Freshman Class of the College.

## COLLEGE

The work of the two college years of the Teachers' Department corresponds somewhat to that of the Freshman and Sophomore years of the College. Eight courses of the College Department of Education may be completed during these two years, thus giving the student that completes the work of the Teachers' Department a very thorough vocational training. The courses in pedagogy, psychology, and the history of education are conducted in accordance with the best normal methods now in vogue. Those completing the work of this department may, after two years' additional work, graduate from the College in the Education Group of studies and receive the Bachelor's degree.

3

**Synopsis of Courses.**—The following is a synopsis of the courses offered in the two college years:

Education 1, 2, 3, 4, 5, 6, 7, 8, and 9 (Eight courses to be taken).
English 1, 2, and 3 (Three courses to be taken).
Mathematics 2 (To be taken).
Chemistry 1, 2, and 3; Biology 1; Physics 1, 2, and 3; Latin 1, 2, 3, and 4; German 1, 2, 3, and 4 (Four courses to be taken).
Bible 1, 2, 3, 4, 5, and 6 (Two courses to be taken).

**Education.**—1. Elementary Psychology. Identical with Psychology 1. Freshman year, fall term.

2. Psychology Applied to Education. Identical with Psychology 2. Freshman year, winter term.

3. History of Education. A study of the educational systems of early China, Greece, and Rome; the history of Christian education; the rise of the universities; the Renaissance; and the educators of the sixteenth, seventeenth, eighteenth, and nineteenth centuries. A careful study is made of such modern educators as Rousseau, Pestalozzi, Froebel, Herbart, and Horace Mann. The last part of the course is devoted to the comparison of the school systems of Germany, France, England, and the United States. Text-book, Monroe's History of Education. Sophomore year, fall term.

4. Child Psychology. Identical with Psychology 3. Sophomore year, winter term.

5. Problems in Secondary Education. The ideals of education and the problems that confront the secondary teacher are carefully studied. The curriculum, discipline, athletics, social organization, sex pedagogy, and the like, as applied to the high school, and kindred subjects are discussed. Text-book, Johnston's High-school Education, supplemented by Hall's Problems in Education, lectures, and reports by the students. Sophomore year, spring term.

6. Teachers' Course in German. Identical with German 10. Open to Sophomores that have had at least one reading course. Junior year, spring term.

7. Teachers' Course in Latin. Identical with Latin 10. Open to Sophomores and Juniors that have had at least one reading course. Senior year, spring term.

8. Educational Psychology. Identical with Psychology 5. Open to Sophomores and Juniors who have completed Psychology 1, 2, and 3. Senior year, spring term.

9. History of Mathematics. Identical with Mathematics 13. Open to Sophomores taking the Teachers' Course. Senior year, spring term.

**Other Courses.**—Detailed descriptions of the other courses offered in the synopsis of the college years of the Teachers' Department will be found under Departments of Instruction in the College Department.

# THE PREPARATORY DEPARTMENT

The purpose of the Preparatory Department is to furnish thorough courses of training in high-school branches leading to entrance to the Freshman Class. Conditioned Freshmen are permitted to make up their conditions in this department. Students in the Teachers' Department take their first four years' work in preparatory courses, and Bible Training students have the privilege of electing studies in this department. Opportunities are provided also for a large and worthy class of young people, with limited means and time at their command, to obtain some preparation for their future work. All the privileges and advantages of the institution are available to students in the Preparatory Department.

## ADMISSION

Admission to the department is by examination. Certificates from principals of secondary schools will, however, be accepted and credit given for equivalent work in any of the subjects required for graduation. Credit thus given is conditional, and will be canceled in any subject in which the student is found to be deficient. Full credit for physiology or physics will not be given unless a reasonable amount of laboratory work has been done in connection with the text-book work. Diplomas must be accompanied by certified statements of the amount of time devoted to each subject studied, and the passing grade, together with the name of the text-book used and the ground covered. Certificates for studies of primary grade and for examinations taken in county normals will not be accepted for credits, but if indorsed by the principal or county superintendent may be accepted as testimonials as to character and general ability. In all cases students coming from other secondary schools, whether asking for credits or not, must present letters of honorable dismissal from their former principals. Students that have been out of school for a number of years are admitted under the general rule that all candidates for admission must furnish satisfactory evidence of good moral character, and must have completed the common-school branches. All students sign a pledge to orderly conduct while members of the institution. Applicants under fifteen years of age, unless residents of Maryville, will not be admitted.

## COURSES OF STUDY

The department offers two courses of study: the Classical and the General. All regular courses of study begin in the fall term and continue throughout the year. Courses may be entered at the opening of the winter or spring term, provided the student has had the work of the preceding term or its equivalent.

## SYNOPSIS OF COURSES

| Classical | General |
|---|---|
| **FIRST YEAR** | **FIRST YEAR** |
| Mathematics II | Mathematics I |
| English I | Mathematics II |
| Latin I | English I |
| History I | History I |
| * Mathematics I | |
| | |
| **SECOND YEAR** | **SECOND YEAR** |
| Mathematics III | Mathematics III |
| English II | English II |
| Latin II | Science I |
| Science I | History II, or |
| * History II | Bookkeeping I |
| | |
| **THIRD YEAR** | **THIRD YEAR** |
| † Mathematics IV | Mathematics IV |
| † English III | English III |
| Latin III | German I, or |
| German I | French I |
| French I | History III |
| History III | |
| | |
| **FOURTH YEAR** | **FOURTH YEAR** |
| ‡ Mathematics V | Mathematics V |
| English IV | English IV |
| Latin IV | German II, or |
| German II | French II |
| French II | Science II |
| Science II | History IV |
| History IV | |

NOTES.—1. English Bible is required for seven weeks each year. The work is so arranged as not to interfere with the other prescribed studies, and is credited for graduation.

2. In addition to the courses listed above, which begin in the fall term, extra classes in Latin I, Mathematics II, and other branches, are provided at the opening of the winter term. For further information see Special Courses and Special Double Courses, in the Teachers' Department, and the smaller bulletins.

* May be taken in addition to the required studies, by permission of the Principal.
† These studies and one language are required; the other study is elected.
‡ The studies to be taken in the fourth year must include Science II and one language; the other two studies are elected.

## REQUIREMENTS FOR GRADUATION

The requirements for graduation in either the Classical or the General Course are fifteen units of work as prescribed in the Synopsis of Courses. A unit is the equivalent of five forty-five-minute recitation periods a week in one subject throughout the academic year. A student may elect either course, but must pursue the studies prescribed in the course elected for at least one year, unless change is made in accordance with the administrative rule regarding changes of course. The prescribed work is four recitation periods a day. All boarding students in this department are required to take gymnasium work to the amount of two hours a week, for which credit for one recitation hour is given. Partial work may be permitted at the discretion of the Principal.

Credits for all work done in this department are recorded on the unit basis. An uncompleted year's work in any subject will be so indicated on the records, and unit credit for that subject withheld until the student shall have completed the year's work. A maximum of one unit condition will be allowed for advancement in classification to the following year. The passing grade in the Preparatory Department is seventy.

## DESCRIPTION OF COURSES

### Mathematics

FIRST YEAR: I. Higher Arithmetic. A thorough course in arithmetic is offered. The subjects considered are percentage and its various applications, exchange, equation of payments, progressions, involution and evolution. mensuration, ratio and proportion, and the metric system.

II. Algebra. The work as given in Milne's New Standard Algebra, to radicals.

SECOND YEAR: III. Algebra. Radicals, quadratics, zero and infinity, ratio and proportion, progressions, logarithms, series, binomial and exponential theorems, indeterminate coefficients, and equations in general.

THIRD YEAR: IV. Plane Geometry. Five books of plane geometry, together with about three hundred original theorems and problems. Wentworth and Smith's Geometry is the text-book used.

FOURTH YEAR: V. Solid Geometry and Plane Trigonometry. Solid Geometry is begun and finished during the fall term. Plane Trigonometry is studied throughout the winter and spring terms. Wentworth and Smith's text-book is used.

### English

FIRST YEAR: I. Technical English Grammar, as presented by the best modern authors, is made the basis of the first year's work. Written themes are required weekly, in which drill is given on capitalization and punctuation, and, in an elementary way, on unity and coherence in the paragraph and the sentence. Special care also is given to the oral work of the student, and oral themes are required. The selections for study are as follows: Halleck and Barbour's Readings from Literature and the First Book of Samuel.

SECOND YEAR: II. Composition and Rhetoric. Brooks' Composition Book II is made the basis of this year's work. Oral and written themes are required weekly. A further study is made of unity and coherence in the composition and in paragraphs, and practice is given in variety of sentence structure. During the year the work is supplemented by the study of selections as follows: The Gospel of Mark; Shakespeare's Julius Cæsar; Scott's Ivanhoe; Selections from American poetry. In addition outside reading is assigned by the teacher in charge.

THIRD YEAR: III. English Literature. During this year written themes are required based on topics that arise from the study of literature and from the daily life of the student. The texts used for study are as follows: Shakespeare's Macbeth; The Four Gospels; Dickens' Tale of Two Cities; Tennyson's Idylls of the King. Reports are required on outside reading assigned by the teacher. In oral work Brewer's Oral English is used.

FOURTH YEAR: IV. English Literature. As a basis of this year's work specimens of the novel, the essay, the drama, the short story, and of poetry are chosen from the classics for special study. The student is required, under the guidance of the teacher, to develop each of these lines of study, with special attention to contemporary literature. Both written and oral themes are required. The classics for study are as follows: Shakespeare's Hamlet; Types of the Short Story (Heydrick); Selections from Wordsworth, Shelley, Keats, Byron, and Browning (Gateway Series); Chaucer's Prologue and Knight's Tale; Emerson's Essays on Manners, Self Reliance, and other subjects; Old Testament Selections.

### Latin

FIRST YEAR: I. First Latin. Pearson's Essentials, supplemented by outlines presented to the class. The First Latin is completed in the spring term, and is followed by the reading of easy prose selections.

SECOND YEAR: II. Cæsar and Latin Composition. Cæsar, four periods each week; Latin composition, one period. During the year outlines are given to the class in its study of Latin grammar. The first four books of the Gallic War are completed. The texts used are Allen and Greenough's Cæsar and Allen and Phillips' Latin Composition.

THIRD YEAR: III. Cicero. Latin Composition. Cicero, four periods each week; Latin composition, one period. The four orations against

Catiline, the Manilian Law, and the Archias. Special attention is paid to drill in pronouncing the Latin, intelligent reading in the original, and translation at sight and at hearing.

FOURTH YEAR: IV. Vergil and Mythology. One month is spent in the study of mythology before beginning Vergil. The principles of quantity and versification are carefully studied. Thorough drill in oral and written scansion. Sight reading. The course covers the first six books of Vergil's Æneid. The last three weeks of the spring term are devoted to prose composition.

### German

THIRD YEAR: I. Grammar, Spanhoofd's Lehrbuch der Deutschen Sprache. This course consists of the principles of German pronunciation, inflection, rules of syntax, the rewriting of easy English sentences in German, and the memorizing of familiar poems. The work of the winter and spring terms is augmented by reading Bacon's Im Vaterland, and Gerstäcker's Irrfahrten.

FOURTH YEAR: II. Grammar, Kaiser and Monteser. This course includes advanced grammar and syntax, use of modes, derivation of words, force of prefixes and suffixes. Some time is devoted to conversation and composition work of an intermediate character. The reading consists of such works of descriptive and narrative prose as will impart facility in translation. Storm's Immensee, Benedix' Die Hochzeitsreise, Gerstäcker's Germelshausen, Mezger and Mueller's Kreuz und Quer, Griltparzer's Der arme Spielmann, Hoffmann's Das Gymnasium zu Holpenburg. Memorizing of longer poems.

### French

THIRD YEAR: I. Elementary French. François' Beginner's French. Composition, conversation, and reading of Guerber's Contes et Legendes, Daudet's Trois Contes Choisis, Erckmann-Chatrian's Madame Thérèse.

FOURTH YEAR: II. Advanced French. Advanced grammar, composition, and conversation, reading selected from such authors as Dumas, Daudet, Sand, About, Schultz, Gréville: La Tulipe Noire, La Belle Nivernaise, La Mère de la Marquise, La Neuvaine de Collette, Dosia. Plays: Scribe's Le Verre d'Eau, Sardou's Les Pattes de Mouche, Molière's Le Bourgeois Gentilhomme.

### History

FIRST YEAR: I. Ancient History. A brief outline of Egyptian and Oriental history from the earliest times to the conquest by Alexander, followed by a fuller course in Greek and Roman history to 476 A. D.

SECOND YEAR: II. Medieval and Modern History. A general survey of European history from the fall of the Western Empire, 476 A. D., to the present time. This work will be centered on the history of France.

THIRD YEAR: III. Advanced United States History and Government. A survey of the history of our country from its beginning to the close of the nineteenth century. This course is designed to give the student a thorough knowledge of the settlement of the country by European colonists in the seventeenth century, the struggle with France for supremacy in America, the cause, course, and consequence of the American Revolution, the development of the Union under the Constitution, the slavery struggle, and the final advance of the country to the position it occupies to-day. Combined with the above, a thorough course in Civics is given, with careful detail of the Constitution and its Amendments. Channing's text is used.

FOURTH YEAR: IV. English History. A brief outline of the history of earlier England, followed by a more careful study of the periods of the Tudors, Stuarts, and House of Brunswick. This course is intended to give the student a good general knowledge of the history of our mother country and to prepare for subsequent courses in English literature and higher United States history.

### Bookkeeping

SECOND YEAR: I. Bookkeeping. Thorough courses conducted throughout the year according to the practical methods employed in business colleges. Students may enter any part of the course in any term. No extra charge is made for this work. The Twentieth Century Bookkeeping is the system used.

### Science

SECOND YEAR: I. General Biology. The purpose of this course is to instruct the student in human physiology and hygiene. The dependence of human life and health on plants and animals is shown by simple demonstrations in plant physiology, followed by similar work in zoology. The principles of physiology thus learned are then applied to man. Three recitation periods and four laboratory periods a week.

FOURTH YEAR: II. Elementary Physics. This course purposes to give the student a knowledge of the fundamental principles of physics and of their applications in every-day life. Three recitation periods and four laboratory periods a week. Text-books, Millikan and Gale's First Course in Physics, and Millikan, Bishop, and Gale's Laboratory Manual.

### English Bible

FIRST YEAR: Studies in the First Book of Samuel. Thirty-five lessons during the winter term. Required in all courses.

SECOND YEAR: Thirty-five lessons in the Gospel of Mark. Required in all courses during the fall term.

THIRD YEAR: The Life of Christ. A text-book adapted to secondary students is used, and the subject is taught so as to prepare for the more advanced course offered in the College Department. Thirty-five lessons during the winter term. Required in all courses.

FOURTH YEAR: A study of Bible characters. Thirty-five lessons during the fall term. Required in all courses.

The Principal will each year arrange the student's hours so that these courses will not conflict with other required courses nor add to the required number of hours a week.

Students are also required to pursue a weekly Bible study in the Bible classes of the Christian Associations of the College or the Sabbath schools of the town.

# THE BIBLE TRAINING DEPARTMENT
## UPON THE JOHN C. MARTIN FOUNDATION

The Bible Training Department provides biblical instruction for all the students enrolled in all other courses of the institution, and offers exceptional advantages for young men and young women wishing to prepare themselves for Christian service as lay workers, Sabbath-school workers, pastors' assistants, mission teachers, or Bible readers.

A three years' course of study is offered. A certificate of graduation will be granted those who, having previously completed fifteen units of high-school work, complete twenty-seven courses selected under the direction of the head of the department from the following groups:

I. Bible Training courses of college grade, all of which are required except those in Bible languages: English Bible, eleven courses; Bible Languages, three courses; and Practical Work, two courses. To these courses, which are described in the ensuing paragraphs, only students prepared to do work of college grade are admitted. Courses are alternated, at least nine being given each year.

II. Other college courses from which supplementary work may be elected: English 1, 2, 3, 12, and 13; Philosophy 2, 3, and 4; Psychology 1, 2, 3, 4, and 5; Social Science 2, 12, and 13; Education 3; History 3; and Spanish 1 and 2; described under the College Department, and Home Economics 1 to 15; described under the Home Economics Department.

III. Preparatory courses from which supplementary work may be elected: Science I; Pedagogy I; and Bookkeeping I. These courses are described under the Preparatory Department.

### ENGLISH BIBLE
#### PROFESSOR GILLINGHAM AND ASSISTANT

1. Life of Christ. The study of the life of Christ is based on a harmony of the Gospels. As an introduction to the course a rapid review of the period between the Testaments is taken, and the principal characteristics of each of the four Gospels are studied. Text-books, Stevens and Burton's Harmony of the Gospels and Burton and Mathews' The Life of Christ. Freshman year, fall term.

2. Pioneers of Palestine. A careful study of Genesis, the geography of Palestine and surrounding countries, and the general mechanics of the Bible. The object of the course is, in addition to the mastery of the subject matter, to develop systematic habits and methods of Bible study. Text-books, the Bible (R. V.), Davis' A Dictionary of the Bible, and the professor's outlines. Reference reading is assigned. Freshman year, winter term.

3. Princes of Palestine. A continuation of Course 2. The work is more rapid, covering Exodus to Ruth. Special attention is paid to the lives and characters of Israel's leaders during this period. Text-books, same as in Course 2. Freshman year, spring term.

4. People of Palestine. A continuation of Course 3, beginning with I Samuel. The national development, the conflicts of Judah and Israel, their governments, their subjugation and partial restoration, their social customs, the character of their leaders, and their influence upon their contemporaries, are studied. An outline course, preparing for detailed treatment of the most important parts in Course 10. Text-books, same as in Course 2. Sophomore year, fall term.

5. The Teachings of Jesus. An analytic and synthetic study based on the words of Jesus as recorded in the Gospels. Use is also made of his works and of the evangelists' comments in helping to determine the nature of Jesus' teaching. James Robertson's Our Lord's Teaching is used also as a text-book. Sophomore year, winter term.

6. The Apostolic Church. A historical study of the early church based on the Acts and Epistles. Text-books, the New Testament (R. V.) and Gilbert's A Short History of Christianity in the Apostolic Age. Sophomore year, spring term.

7. A Bird's-eye View of the Bible. This course treats very briefly General and Particular Introduction, and brings the entire Bible before the student in rapid review. Text-books, Robertson's The Old Testament and Its Contents and M'Clymont's The New Testament and Its Writers. Junior year, fall term.

8. Poets of Palestine. An outline study of Job, Proverbs, Ecclesiastes, Song of Solomon, and selected Psalms. Introductory lectures on Hebrew poetry and wisdom literature. Portions of the books are studied in detail and their relation to other sacred literature and their importance in Christian experience are emphasized. No commentaries are used as text-books, but required readings are assigned; and the professor furnishes a syllabus of each book. Junior year, winter term.

9. Prophets of Palestine. The methods outlined in Course 8 are followed. The prophecies are reviewed chronologically in the light of

contemporaneous history. Messianic prophecy is given special attention. Junior year, spring term.

10. Men and Messages of the Old Testament. A search study for advanced students. The great leaders of Israel and their messages are carefully studied. In 1916-1917, Elijah, Elisha, Isaiah, Jeremiah, Ezekiel, the twelve minor prophets, and Ezra and Nehemiah were studied. Commentaries suitable to the nature of the work are used. Senior year, fall term.

11. Men and Messages of the New Testament. A search study for advanced students. This alternates with Course 10 and pursues the same method of study, with word analysis based on Vincent's Word Studies in the New Testament. Senior year, fall term.

### BIBLE LANGUAGES
#### Professors Gillingham and Davis

12, 13. Hebrew. Identical with Hebrew 1, 2. Senior year, fall and winter terms.—Professor Gillingham.

14. Greek Testament. Identical with Greek 11. Sophomore year, spring term.—Professor Davis.

### PRACTICAL WORK
#### Professor Gillingham

17. Bible Teaching: Principles and Practice. This course has reference especially to personal work and the conducting of Bible classes. The organization and management of the Sabbath school are studied. Lectures, quizzes, preparation of Bible lessons for teaching, and practice under the direction of the instructor. Sophomore year, winter term.

18. Religious Address: Principles and Practice. Preparation for religious services, missionary programs, and the like; selection and development of themes; sources and use of illustrations; addresses on special occasions and to special audiences; and drill in the reading of hymns and passages of Scripture. As much practical work is done by the student as possible. Sophomore year, spring term.

### COURSES FOR PREPARATORY STUDENTS
#### Miss Alexander and Miss Clemens

For First Year students: Studies in the First Book of Samuel; thirty-five lessons. For Second Year students: The Gospel of Mark; thirty-five lessons. For Third Year students: The Life of Christ; thirty-five lessons. For Fourth Year students: A study of Bible characters; thirty-five lessons.

# THE HOME ECONOMICS DEPARTMENT

The liberality of an anonymous donor, who contributed the Mary Esther Memorial Endowment Fund, made it possible in 1913 for the College to add a Home Economics Department to the privileges already afforded its students. The principal home of the department is the third story of Fayerweather Science Hall, which was added to the building in 1913 by the generosity of the founder of the department as an additional memorial of her mother. The large and well-lighted rooms have been equipped in the most recent and approved manner, through the kindness of the same generous lady. Spacious rooms are set aside as sewing-room, kitchen, dining-room, lecture-room, and general room. The hospital is also employed in connection with the teaching of home nursing and sanitation, and rooms in the dormitories in connection with the teaching of housekeeping. The home economics courses in chemistry are given in the chemistry laboratories and lecture-room. The courses scheduled in this department are offered without extra tuition. A small laboratory fee is charged for the use of equipment, and in the sewing classes students provide their own materials as specified in the description of courses. All articles made in the sewing classes are exhibited at the end of the term, and at the close of the annual exhibit are returned to the student. Cotton dresses should be worn in the laboratories, and long white aprons with bibs are required.

Preparatory students may enter such classes of the Home Economics Department as are adapted to their degree of advancement, and will be allowed in this department a maximum credit of two units toward the fifteen units required for graduation from the Preparatory Department. College students pursuing college grade studies in this department will be allowed three credits in home economics toward the seven science electives required to complete the total of thirty-six credits necessary for graduation with the B.A. degree in the Science Group.

For students that desire to take all their studies in this department, two-year and three-year courses are offered. Fifteen recitation hours a week for thirty-six weeks constitute a year's work. Two hours of laboratory practice count as one recitation hour. Students that do not wish to take the three-year course may receive a certificate for the completion of two years' work. Both preparatory and college students are eligible to these certificates. Students that wish to prepare for teaching the subject will be required to pursue the full course of three years. Diplomas will be granted students of college standing that complete twenty-seven courses selected under the direction of the head of the department from the following groups:

I.  Home Economics courses, nine of which are required for graduation, as follows: 1, 2, 3, 4, 5, 6, 7, 8, 9, 10, 11, 12, 13, 14, and 15.

II.  College courses as follows: Chemistry 1, 2, 11, and 12 (three must be taken); Education 1, 2, 3, 4, 5, and 8 (two must be taken); English 1, 2, and 3; and Bible 1, 2, 3, 4, 5, and 6 (two must be taken). These courses are described under the College Department.

III.  Preparatory courses as follows: Pedagogy I (three terms); Science I (three terms); Science II (three terms); and Bookkeeping I (at least one term). These are to be taken unless substituted for from among the higher courses offered above. These courses are described under the Preparatory Department.

Special classes in cooking, if called for, will be organized for students from Maryville and vicinity who may wish to take only this work.

## HOME ECONOMICS

### Miss Ryland and Miss Trent

1, 2, 3.  Cookery and Clothing.  Elementary studies intended for those that have had no previous training in the subjects taught. The courses consist of the following work: (a) Foods and Cookery. The purpose of this course is to give practice in fundamental cooking processes in order to develop skill and efficiency in handling food materials and cooking utensils. It includes the study of food materials, principles of cookery, care of food in the house, how to study the recipe, methods of mixing, the making of beverages, vegetables and vegetable cookery, cereals, proteins — eggs, milk, cheese, fats — batters and doughs, salads, and simple desserts. Bacteria, yeasts, and molds of the household are studied two hours a week throughout the fall term as part of the work in Course 1. The instruction in bacteriology is given by Miss Green, in the biological laboratory. Textbooks, Kinne and Cooley's Foods and Household Management, and Conne's Bacteria, Yeasts, and Molds in the Home. (b) Textiles and Clothing. Elementary clothing and handwork. As a preliminary to the practical work specified below, students are taught, as needed, the various stitches used in garment making, machine stitching, and the use and care of the sewing-machine and attachments. During the year the students make the following articles from materials which they provide, subject to the approval of the instructor, at the approximate cost of eight dollars: two pieces of underclothing, made by hand; a nightgown and a laundry bag, made by hand and machine; a slip, a plain shirtwaist or middy, and a plain tailored cotton skirt, made by machine. The students also make a simple muslin dress, and embroider a towel, a table runner, and a centerpiece. The articles thus made are the property of the student. In this course darning and patching are taught. Pattern drafting is also taught, and the students draft patterns for a kimono nightgown and a plain skirt. Text-book, Kinne and Cooley's Shelter and Clothing. These three courses are required for certificate or diploma. Laboratory practice in cooking, four hours a week, in sewing, four hours; recitation, one hour. Fall, winter, and spring terms.

4, 5, 6. Cookery and Clothing. (a) Foods and Cookery. Home cookery and table service. This course consists of a review of food principles and the theory of cookery; the preparation of more elaborate dishes; the study of meats, soups, canning, and frozen desserts; the planning and serving of simple meals; and a study of the comparative cost and nutritive value of different food materials. Text-book, Snyder's Human Foods, and references to government bulletins. (b) Textiles and Clothing. · Drafting and elementary dressmaking. This course includes drafting, cutting, and fitting. Shirtwaists, plain skirts, and sleeves are cut in cambric from drafted patterns, and fitted. The patterns are then altered, and the articles to be made are cut from the altered patterns. Practice is given in testing commercial patterns. During the year the students make the following articles of clothing from materials which they provide, subject to the approval of the instructor, at the approximate cost of fifteen dollars: a tailored shirtwaist and skirt, a simple muslin dress, an unlined silk dress, and a wool skirt. The garments thus made are the property of the student. These three courses are required for certificate or diploma. Prerequisites, Home Economics 1, 2, and 3, or equivalents. Laboratory practice in cooking, four hours a week, in sewing, four hours; recitation, one hour. Fall, winter, and spring terms.

7, 8, 9. Cookery. These courses consist of all the work offered in Courses 1, 2, 3, 4, 5, and 6 on the subject of Cookery. They are intended for students already proficient in sewing, or who, for reasons satisfactory to the head of the department, do not desire instruction in sewing and are able to take both years of Cookery at the same time. Laboratory practice in cooking, eight hours a week; recitation, one hour. Fall, winter, and spring terms.

10, 11, 12. Clothing. These courses consist of all the work offered in Courses 1, 2, 3, 4, 5, and 6 on the subject of Clothing. They are intended for students already proficient in cooking, or who, for reasons satisfactory to the head of the department, do not desire instruction in cooking, and are able to take both years of Clothing at the same time. Laboratory practice in sewing and drafting, eight hours a week; recitation, one hour. Fall, winter, and spring terms.

13, 14, 15. Cookery, Housekeeping, and Home Nursing. These courses consist of: (a) Cookery. The various methods of preserving and canning.

Invalid cookery. Demonstration cookery. Lunch-room cookery. The preparation and serving of typical and economical luncheon dishes. The five-cent and ten-cent luncheon are considered with reference to schools. History of cookery. Text-book, Sherman's Chemistry of Food and Nutrition, and Rose's Laboratory Manual of Dietetics. (b) Housekeeping. Household management. Discussions and readings. This course includes the questions of the budget, the cost of living, problems of household labor, the care of children, and the social side of home life. Household furnishings. The decoration and furnishing of the entire house, artistic and economic furnishing, cost of materials and labor, and visits to house-furnishing establishments. History of the family and home-making. (c) Home Nursing. General structure of the body. General instruction for care of sickness in the home. Bed-making. Bathing. Food. Medicine and general treatment. Care of infants and children. Infectious diseases. Emergencies and first aid. (d) Sewing. Making of a layette. Tailoring. Dyeing and renovating. (e) Basketry. These three courses are required for diploma. Prerequisites, Home Economics 1, 2, 3, 4, 5, and 6, and Chemistry 1, 2, and 11, or equivalents. Laboratory practice in cooking, four hours a week; recitations, three hours. Fall, winter, and spring terms.

Courses will be added also in the subjects of practice teaching, textiles, history of costume, laundering, and shelter, as the growth of the department demands.

THE DEDICATION OF THE SERVICE FLAG

# THE AGRICULTURAL DEPARTMENT

For a number of years the needs of public-school teachers for elementary training in agriculture were met by a short text-book course offered in the Preparatory Department. This course had, however, become entirely inadequate, and in 1916 a separate department was established. The preparation of the one hundred acres that are to be devoted to the work of this department has continued during the past year. Equipment in the matter of stock and necessary barns, silos, and the like sufficient to meet the needs of the present courses offered has been provided, and funds for additional equipment and endowment to permit the full development of the department are being sought. A herd of registered Holstein cattle has been begun. Advanced courses will be offered as needed, and sufficient work given to provide, in connection with supplemental studies, a three years' course in agriculture. Complete or partial work in this department will be very helpful to public-school teachers, and care is taken to make the department meet their practical needs. The courses offered also prepare for advanced work in the respective branches in university schools of agriculture. Credit is given in the Preparatory Department for any course taken in agriculture, and college credit will be allowed for specified courses when taken by students of college grade and with the special additional library, laboratory, and field-work required by the head of the department.

## AGRICULTURE

### Mr. Hopkins

I. Elements of Agriculture. A text-book course for students of preparatory, or high-school, grade, and corresponding to the studies of the fourth year. Laboratory and field-work supplement the text. Prerequisite, Science I. Laboratory practice and field-work, four hours a week; recitations, three hours. Fall, winter, and spring terms.

1, 2, 3. Fundamentals of Agriculture. A beginning course for students of college grade. The subjects studied are, the improvement of plants and animals, propagation of plants, plant food, soil, fertility of the land, important farm crops, systems of cropping, farm animals, feeds and feeding, farm management, the farm home, the farm community. Special assignments for investigation, with reference work in government bulletins and works especially treating the several subjects given in the text-book. Themes on subjects investigated. Practical work, farm and garden, dairying, orchard pruning, corn testing, seed selection, and the like. Prerequisite, not less than fourteen standard units, including one year in elementary botany or general biology. Laboratory practice and field-work, four to six hours; recitations, three to two hours. Fall, winter, and spring terms.

4

# THE DEPARTMENT OF MUSIC

It is the purpose of this department to lay a firm technical foundation that will lead to the expression of the highest musical thought and emotion. The works of the best masters are employed through all grades, so that the pupil may grow continually in musical taste and may develop a sympathetic comprehension of all that enters into artistic performance. The study of Harmony, Theory, and History of Music is urged. Pupils are required to read and pass examinations upon reference works, provided in the Library, as assigned by the teachers. Lectures are given during the year by the head of the department on the subject of Musical Appreciation. Compositions are played and analyzed, and an effort is made to point out their underlying thought and meaning. These lectures are open to the general public as well as to students of the College. Monthly recitals also are given by the students of the department in the chapel auditorium.

On account of the individual needs of the pupil, it is considered inadvisable to adhere too persistently to any special set of exercises and studies, but advisable, rather, to select those that will meet the particular requirements of each pupil. A general idea of the various courses may be had by the following outlines.

## PIANO

### Miss Hale and Assistants

Elementary Course. Building up the hand. Correcting improper or faulty hand positions, and the reinforcing of the hand by means of exercises. Training in a knowledge of notes, their relationship to the keyboard, rhythm, and the like. Studies and sonatas selected from the works of Czerny, Bertini, Clementi, Handel, Mozart, and Beethoven, supplemented by easy pieces from modern composers, such as Schumann, Schytté, Reinecke, and Scharwenka.

Intermediate Course. More difficult forms of scale, including major and minor scales, scales in thirds, sixths, and tenths; broken chords and arpeggios with their inversions; dominant and diminished seventh chords in their different positions. Studies of considerable technical difficulty from the works of Czerny, Berens, and Cramer. Emphasis on the study of Bach's two-part and three-part Inventions. Classical compositions, including sonatas, from the works of Beethoven, Mozart, and Haydn. Study of the best modern compositions. By the end of the Intermediate Course pupils must be able to play at least five compositions from memory.

ADVANCED COURSE. Studies of technical difficulty, including "Gradus ad Parnassum," Clementi, Moscheles, and Chopin; also compositions by Beethoven, Schumann, Mendelssohn, and others, supplemented by those of the best modern composers. Pupils in this course are required to appear several times in recital, playing from memory whatever compositions are selected. It is also necessary to cover the requirements in Harmony and History of Music, and to take the course in Normal Training. When the pupil has done the work of this course successfully, he is entitled to a diploma in Piano, and upon graduation will be assisted in securing a position by the college agency, the Committee on Recommendations, if so desired.

### VOICE
#### MISS STAATER

Correct breathing and breath control. Placing of the voice and development of the resonance. Training of the ear and mind. Enunciation and diction. Vocalises such as Vaccai, Sieber, Martzo (Preparatory and Advanced), and Lütgen. Song interpretation. Répertoire work, including the Classics, German Lieder, Opera, and Oratorio.

All vocal students are required to take Sight-singing, Theory, and History of Music. The requirements in Harmony, Theory, and History of Music are the same for graduation in Voice as those required in Piano. In addition, the pupil must be able to sing in at least one language besides his own.

### VIOLIN
#### MR. TEDFORD

Private instruction is given to each pupil. Dancla's method is used for beginners, followed by Schradieck's and Kayser's Scale and Technical Studies, together with solo selections. Ensemble work is made a regular exercise in the college orchestra, which meets each week and plays for many of the public entertainments and chapel exercises.

### MUSICAL ORGANIZATIONS

CHORUS AND CHOIR. Instruction is given free to any students desiring to take the work of chorus and choir singing and sight reading.

GLEE CLUBS. Separate clubs for male voices and female voices are organized by the teacher of voice, and are accessible to those that have a fair knowledge of the rudiments of vocal music.

ORCHESTRA. Opportunity to become a member of the orchestra is given to any students having sufficient musical training

BAND. The band is composed entirely of students in this institution, and is open to any student possessing a fair knowledge of band music.

# THE DEPARTMENT OF ART

The work of this department is designed to train the hand and the eye, and to cultivate the æsthetic sense, thereby adding to the student's cultural equipment and increasing his abilities along every line of endeavor. The courses offered, here described in outline, may be varied to meet the needs of individual pupils and the growth of the department.

## FREE-HAND DRAWING
### Miss Smith

Class lessons in free-hand drawing are available to students of all the other departments without extra charges. These lessons are designed to lay a foundation for work on industrial and artistic lines. The student is taught to draw from still-life objects, including casts, and from nature.

## FINE ARTS
### Miss Smith

A short course, covering two years, is offered especially for school teachers, though open to all students. During the first year the work includes an elementary study of design and color; free-hand drawing; simple perspective; lettering and blackboard work; and the study of pictures. Pencil, ink, crayola, and water color are used. The pupil is required to submit for exhibition, four applied designs; four studies in still life; and two examples of lettering. During the second year the work includes the study of design and space filling as applied to school work; interior decoration and textiles; perspective and free-hand drawing; further study of pictures; study of color in still life and landscapes; and the history of art. The pupil is required to submit for exhibition, four designs to illustrate school work and home interior; four applied textile designs; two perspective drawings; and four paintings in still life and landscape.

A special course covering three years is offered to those desiring to carry on more extended studies. Certificates of proficiency are granted to those students who, after at least three years' study, have proved themselves entitled to them. The work of the first year includes a study of structural form; light and dark masses in objects; still-life groups and landscape; simple compositions and color work; perspective and memory problems; and the study of pictures. The mediums used are charcoal, crayola, water color, and oil. The pupil submits for exhibition, four studies illustrating structural form, in black and white; four still-life groups, in black and white or in oils; and four landscapes. In the second year studies are conducted in elementary design; modeling, to aid in the study of form; drawing and painting from still life, landscape, and life; composition and picture study, with memory work; and the history of art. The pupil submits for exhibition two original designs; four landscapes in color; four still-life groups; four sketches from the costumed model; and one original composition. The third year's work includes modeling and drawing from cast and from life; design as applied to textiles, metals, or block-printing; landscape and outdoor figure sketching; advanced still-life work; color theory and perspective; composition and picture study; and the history of art. The pupil submits for exhibition, a head modeled from cast or from life; four applied original designs; four landscapes; two still-life groups; and two sketches from life.

A fourth year of study for students that have obtained the certificate of proficiency is provided. During this year the studies include modeling from life; work from costumed model; pen and ink sketching; portrait and figure painting; and compositions with landscapes and figures from memory and imagination. The pupil is required to prepare an exhibit of at least twenty pieces, including a figure or head modeled from life; a painted portrait or figure; landscape with figures; and an imaginative composition.

Courses in poster designing and special courses in design as applied to textiles, metals, leather, and basketry may be arranged for by pupils that have had the first year of the short course or its equivalent. A course in illustrating may be arranged for by pupils that have had the first year of the special course or its equivalent. Arrangements may also be made for a course in bookbinding by those desiring it.

# THE DEPARTMENT OF EXPRESSION AND PUBLIC SPEAKING

This department offers courses of study designed to meet the needs of those that desire to become teachers of reading and public speaking or to develop greater effectiveness as platform readers or public speakers. The aim is to cultivate the power to appreciate and interpret standard literature, and to secure simplicity and naturalness in the development of individual powers of expression. To this end the individual needs of each pupil are studied, and special pains are taken to prevent affectation and artificiality. The methods pursued are not imitative but creative, and embody practice in rendering selections from the best standard authors, and in outlining, preparing, and delivering orations.

A three years' course of study is offered. A diploma of graduation will be granted in either Expression or in Public Speaking to those who, having fifteen units of preparatory or high-school work, including at least two units of foreign language and four units of English, complete the courses as outlined.

College students not desiring to take the full course in Expression or in Public Speaking may receive credit for work taken in this department as follows: Three terms of individual weekly lessons in Expression or in Public Speaking, with their required hour of practice each day, taken by students of college rank, shall, when completed, receive credit on the college records as equivalent to a one term's regular course of study, and shall be entered on the records as "Public Speaking." Not more than two such credits shall, however, be allowed.

## EXPRESSION

### Mrs. West and Miss Buxton

1. Natural Drills in Expression. Voice culture, including physiology of the vocal organs, correct breathing, tone support, responsiveness of the voice, correcting defects of voice, articulation, and pronunciation. Physical culture for grace and poise in expression, gesture, and pantomime. Individual training and practice. Text-book, Phillips' Natural Drills in Expression. Individual lesson, one hour a week; practice, five hours a week; class lesson, one hour a week; gymnasium drill, two hours a week. First year, fall, winter, and spring terms.

2. Bible Reading and Shakespeare. Class work in these branches throughout the year. Voice culture and physical culture as outlined for

the first year's course. Individual training and practice of advanced grade. Individual lesson, one hour a week; practice, five hours a week; class lesson, one hour a week; gymnasium drill, two hours a week. Second year, fall, winter, and spring terms.

3. Dramatization. Class work throughout the year. Literary criticism and story telling, two terms. Voice culture and physical culture continued. Individual training and practice of advanced grade continued. Individual lesson, one hour a week; practice, five hours a week; class lesson, one hour a week; gymnasium drill, two hours a week. Third year, fall, winter, and spring terms.

The following college courses, English 1, 2, 3, 5, and 6, and Psychology 1, must also be taken before graduation.

## PUBLIC SPEAKING
MRS. WEST AND ASSOCIATE PROFESSOR SOUTHWICK

1. Natural Drills in Expression. This course is the same as Course 1 in Expression, except in the kind of individual lessons given. Text-book, Phillips' Effective Speaking. Individual lesson, one hour a week; practice, five hours a week; class lesson, one hour a week; gymnasium drill, two hours a week. First year, fall, winter, and spring terms.

2. Bible Reading and Shakespeare. This course is the same as Course 2 in Expression, except in the kind of individual lessons given. Individual lesson, one hour a week; practice, five hours a week; class lesson, one hour a week; gymnasium drill, two hours a week. Second year, fall, winter, and spring terms.

3. Public Speaking. In place of the methods pursued in Courses 1 and 2, the college courses in Public Speaking, English 12 and 13, are taken. In connection with this course of study there is individual training provided in preparation for interclass, intersociety, and intercollegiate debates and oratorical contests. For the description of English 12 and 13 see English Language in the College Department. Third year, fall and winter terms.

The following additional college courses, English 1, 2, 3, 5, and 6, and Psychology 1, must also be taken before graduation.

# GENERAL INFORMATION

## HISTORY

In "A Century of Maryville College — A Story of Altruism," written by President Wilson, and published by The Directors in 1916, has been gathered an ample record of the first one hundred years of the institution's life. A fuller statement regarding the book will be found elsewhere in this catalog. In the following paragraphs the history of the College is recorded in brief.

Maryville College, like most of the older colleges, grew out of the zeal that the pioneers of the American church had for the education of the people. The same year (1802) in which Isaac Anderson was ordained to the ministry by the Presbytery of Union, he founded within the bounds of his Grassy Valley congregation, near Knoxville, a school which he called "Union Academy," but which was popularly known as "the Log College." He built for it a large four-roomed log house. In this, for the times, pretentious building, many men who afterwards served their country well were educated. Among this number was Governor Reynolds, of Illinois. Dr. Anderson in 1812 removed to Maryville and took charge of New Providence Church, of which organization he remained pastor till his death, which took place in 1857. In Maryville he continued his academic work. The most famous pupil of this Maryville academy was Sam Houston, who afterward had so unique and picturesque a career as general, governor, president of Texas, congressman, and patriot.

Dr. Anderson, however, felt that more should be done toward providing an educated ministry for the Southwest. Encouraged by others like-minded with himself, he founded Maryville College in 1819. The institution was born of the moral and spiritual needs of the early settlers of East Tennessee — chiefly Scotch-Irish Presbyterians — and was designed principally to educate for the ministry men who should be native to the soil. The grand motive of the founder may be stated in his own words: "LET THE DIRECTORS AND MANAGERS OF THIS SACRED INSTITUTION PROPOSE THE GLORY OF GOD AND THE ADVANCEMENT OF THAT KINGDOM PURCHASED BY THE BLOOD OF HIS ONLY BEGOTTEN SON AS THEIR SOLE OBJECT." Inspired by such a motive, Dr. Anderson gathered a class of five candidates for the ministry in the fall of 1819, and in prayer and faith began what proved to be the principal work of his life. In forty-two years the institution put one hundred and fifty men into the ministry. Its endowment, gathered by littles through all these years, was only sixteen thousand dollars.

Then came the Civil War, and suspended the work of the institution for five years, and the College came out of the general wreck with little save its good name and precious history.

After the war the Synod of Tennessee, moved by the spirit of self-preservation, and by a desire to promote Christian education in the Central South, resolved to revive Maryville College. The institution was reopened in 1866. New grounds and new buildings were an imperative necessity. To meet this need, sixty-five thousand dollars was secured, and the College was saved from extinction. The consequent growth was so great that the securing of an endowment also became a necessity. Professor Thomas Jefferson Lamar, the second founder of the College, took up the great task of securing this endowment, and labored with unceasing toil and self-denial until success was attained. In response to his appeal, in 1883, a few generous friends — William Thaw, William E. Dodge, Preserved Smith, Dr. Sylvester Willard, and others — contributed an endowment fund of one hundred thousand dollars. During the canvass for the fund, Professor Lamar lost his only child by death. This loss and the strain of the canvass proved so heavy a burden that his health failed, and two years later he passed away. In 1891, Daniel Fayerweather, counseled by Dr. Hitchcock, a friend of President Bartlett and Professor Lamar, bequeathed to the College the sum of one hundred thousand dollars, and also made it one of twenty equal participants in the residuary estate. The College received two hundred and sixteen thousand dollars by the provisions of the will. This magnificent donation enabled the institution to enlarge its work and to enter upon a new era of usefulness and influence. On January 1, 1905, Mr. Ralph Voorhees, of New Jersey, made the munificent donation of one hundred thousand dollars to the general endowment fund of the College. The gift is subject to a five per cent annuity during the lifetime of Mrs. Voorhees. The reception of this superb benefaction filled the hearts of Maryville's friends with confidence, and with intense gratitude to God and to God's stewards.

In 1906, the rapid growth in the number of students having made necessary much further enlargement of the teaching force and of the material equipment of the institution, President Wilson entered upon a campaign for additional endowment. Mr. Andrew Carnegie generously offered the College twenty-five thousand dollars on condition that fifty thousand dollars additional be secured. In 1907, the General Education Board pledged fifty thousand dollars on condition that one hundred and fifty thousand dollars be secured from other sources. Mr. Carnegie then increased his pledge to fifty thousand dollars toward this larger fund. The time limit set for the completion of the fund was December 31, 1908. In the face of many difficulties the President, with reliance upon the favor of God, prosecuted the campaign for the "Forward Fund of Two Hundred Thousand

Dollars." In order to meet the spirit as well as the letter of the requirements of the conditional pledges, it was deemed necessary to raise twenty-five thousand dollars more than the designated sum. When the canvass closed, the subscriptions amounted to the splendid sum of two hundred and twenty-seven thousand dollars. The fact that, in spite of the recent panic and hard times, the uneasiness of a presidential year, and the ill health of the canvasser, the "Forward Fund" was secured, filled the Faculty, Directors, and friends of the College with a deep sense of gratitude to God, and to his human agents who took part with Maryville in its ministry to the noble youth of mountain and valley in its Southern Appalachian field.

During the past nine years there have been, besides a steady increase of the permanent scholarship funds and numerous contributions for minor but pressing needs of the College, three notable advances made: (1) by the gift of an endowment of sixteen thousand dollars by an anonymous donor, a Home Economics Department has been established; (2) by the gift of thirteen thousand and five hundred dollars by the late Louis H. Severance, Esq., a third story has been added to Pearsons Hall, providing dormitory room for fifty additional young women; and (3) by the additional gift of twelve thousand dollars by the anonymous donor of the Mary Esther Home Economics endowment fund, it has been possible for the College to add a third story to Fayerweather Science Hall in order to provide quarters for the Home Economics Department.

As the result of the generous contributions made through many years by many philanthropic donors, the College now owns property and endowment to the total amount of over one million dollars. Of this amount, about five hundred thousand dollars is invested in endowment and the remainder in buildings and equipment.

Three hundred and seven of the alumni have entered the ministry, while fifty-two post-bellum alumni and undergraduates have been or are missionaries in Japan, China, Siam, Korea, India, Persia, Syria, Africa, the Philippines, Colombia, Chile, Mexico, Cuba, and Porto Rico. Several are laboring in missions in the West. All the alumni are engaged in honorable pursuits. Students who have gone from the College to the theological, medical, and legal schools have usually attained a high rank in their classes. A goodly number of the alumni are now studying in theological seminaries.

The necessary expenses are so phenomenally low as to give the institution a special adaptation to the middle class and to the struggling poor of valley and mountain — the great mass of the surrounding population — and to young people of other sections of the country where the cost of attending college is beyond their ability to defray.

The privileges of the institution are, of course, open alike to all young men and young women of good moral character irrespective of their religious affiliation. All the leading denominations are largely represented **in the student body.**

## LOCATION

Maryville is a pleasant and thriving town of about eight thousand inhabitants. It is widely known as "the town of schools and churches." It is sixteen miles south of Knoxville. There are four trains a day each way on the Knoxville and Augusta Railroad, two trains each way on the Louisville and Nashville Railroad, and one train each way on the Tennessee and Carolina Southern Railroad.

Maryville is an ideal health resort for students from other States. The town lies on the hills, one thousand feet above sea level, and enjoys the life-giving breezes from the Chilhowees and the Smokies, a few miles away. Young people from the North and other sections are greatly benefited in health by a year at Maryville, and many take their entire course here.

## COLLEGE STATION POST OFFICE

A branch of the United States post office at Maryville has been established on the campus and is located in Anderson Hall. All of the usual post office conveniences are furnished. Mail is delivered to the dormitories and offices. Students should have their mail addressed, College Station, Maryville, Tennessee, adding the name of the dormitory in which they room, and, in the case of young men in Carnegie Hall, the room number also.

## GROUNDS AND BUILDINGS

The college grounds consist of two hundred and fifty acres, and for beautiful scenery are not surpassed by any in the country. They are elevated and undulating, covered with a beautiful growth of evergreens and with a noble forest, and command a splendid view of the Cumberland Mountains on the north, and of the Smoky Mountains on the south. The location is as remarkable for its healthfulness as it is for its beauty. The campus affords the choicest facilities for the development of athletics.

On these grounds there are sixteen buildings, which, together with the grounds and equipment, represent an investment of nearly five hundred thousand dollars. The buildings are heated with steam and lighted with electricity from the central power plant on the campus. Generous contributions from several givers have enabled the College to begin the installation of a new water system. The water rights to some protected springs situated a mile and a half from the college grounds have been obtained, and pipes have been laid connecting these springs with the pipes of the old water system, through which the water is pumped by electrical power to the reservoir tank on the campus. It is thence conveyed to all the dormitories, the gymnasium, the swimming pool, the fountain, and the science laboratories, supplying an abundance of pure water for drinking as well as for toilet facilities. A fifty thousand gallon steel tank has supplanted the old tanks formerly in use. As soon as funds are provided for the purpose, additional toilet facilities will be furnished in the recitation buildings, and additional sanitary drinking fountains will be installed in all the buildings and on the campus. The buildings, except two cottages used for residences, are more fully described in the following paragraphs.

ANDERSON HALL, the central building, is the oldest of the present college halls, having been built in 1869, and named in honor of the founder of the institution. It contains the administrative offices and most of the recitation rooms for the literary departments. The large addition to the Hall, the Fayerweather Annex, is occupied by the Preparatory Department.

BALDWIN HALL, named in honor of the late John C. Baldwin, of New Jersey, is a dormitory for young women. It contains rooms for one hundred and forty students. It is provided, as are all the dormitories, with all modern conveniences, and is a comfortable homes for young women.

MEMORIAL HALL, originally built as a companion building to Baldwin Hall, is a young men's dormitory, containing rooms for seventy students. While it is one of the oldest of the college buildings, it is kept in excellent repair, and is a comfortable and well-equipped dormitory. It is under the control of a regular officer of the College.

WILLARD MEMORIAL, the home of the President, was provided in 1890 by a generous gift of Mrs. Jane F. Willard, in memory of her husband, Sylvester Willard, M.D. It is one of the chief adornments of the campus, and is a valuable property.

THE LAMAR MEMORIAL LIBRARY HALL was erected in 1888 at a cost of five thousand five hundred dollars, which amount was generously provided by three friends of Professor Lamar and of the College. The building is a noble and fitting monument. The large memorial window contributed by the brothers and sisters of Professor Lamar holds the central position.

BARTLETT HALL is one of the largest college Y. M. C. A. buildings in the South. Planned for by the students led by Kin Takahashi, a Japanese student, it was erected by contributions made or secured by the Bartlett Hall Building Association, supplemented by a large appropriation by the college authorities. A liberal donation made by Mrs. Nettie F. McCormick in 1901 enabled the committee to complete the building. In 1911, Mrs. Elizabeth R. Voorhees made a generous gift providing for extensive alterations and improvements, including the building of a separate gymnasium for the use of young women. The Y. M. C. A. auditorium. parlors, and secretary's and committees' apartments occupy the front part of the building, while the large gymnasiums occupy the rest of the structure.

FAYERWEATHER SCIENCE HALL was erected in 1898 through the liberal bequest of Daniel B. Fayerweather. The building as erected was two stories in height, with extreme dimensions of one hundred and six feet by ninety-seven feet. The first floor contains spacious laboratories for chemistry and physics, a lecture-room, storerooms, an office, and the John C. Branner Scientific Library. The second floor contains four excellent lecture-rooms, two large and well-lighted laboratories for physics and agriculture, and the laboratory of experimental psychology. The laboratories are furnished with both direct and alternating electric current, and also with gas. The building is thoroughly modern in every respect. It is provided with liberal equipment for the practical study of science, and will stand a useful and lasting monument to the intelligent philanthropy of the princely giver whose name it bears. In 1913 the anonymous donor of the Mary Esther Memorial Fund that provided for the establishment of the Home Economics Department, also contributed funds for the building of the third and fourth floors of this hall for the housing of the Home Economics Department, as an additional memorial of her mother. The third floor contains, besides cloak-rooms, storerooms, closets, toilets, and lockers, a reading-room, dining-room, kitchen, sewing-room, lecture-room, and one small and one large laboratory. On the fourth floor are three large rooms for general purposes.

THE ELIZABETH R. VOORHEES CHAPEL was erected in 1905-1906 by gifts made by the late Mr. Ralph Voorhees, of New Jersey, and by other donors. The chapel, named in honor of Mrs. Voorhees, graces one of the most commanding sites on the grounds, and is well worthy of its place of distinction. The auditorium seats eight hundred and eighty persons and can be arranged to accommodate two or three hundred more. The basement contains seventeen well-lighted rooms, occupied by the Music Department, and a commodious auditorium occupied by the Y. W. C. A. To the rear of the main auditorium, also, and on the floor above, are several rooms used by the Department of Expression and for various other purposes.

THE RALPH MAX LAMAR MEMORIAL HOSPITAL, named in honor of Mrs. Lamar's only son, who died in infancy, was built in 1909 through the generosity of Mrs. Martha A. Lamar, a life-long friend of the College. Her gift of six thousand dollars provided a thoroughly modern hospital building, containing eleven wards, caretakers' rooms, baths, toilets, an operating-room, and other appointments of a well-ordered hospital. A gift of five hundred dollars from the late Mr. Nathaniel Tooker, of East Orange, N. J., together with about five hundred dollars from other sources, secured the purchase of a valuable outfit of the best hospital furnishings and medical supplies.

CARNEGIE HALL.—In connection with the "Forward Fund" secured in 1908, Mr. Andrew Carnegie gave the sum of fifty thousand dollars for a dormitory for young men. The building was occupied at the opening of the fall term in 1910, and was dedicated on January 11, 1911. On April 12, 1916, the building was totally destroyed by the only serious fire occurring in the history of the College. The insurance of thirty thousand dollars was promptly paid, and preparations for rebuilding were immediately begun. On May 4, 1916, the Maryville Chamber of Commerce, through a committee of sixty leading business men, undertook to raise a rebuilding fund of twenty-five thousand dollars among the citizens of Maryville and Blount County. Of this amount, the faculty of the College subscribed five thousand dollars. The new building was completed in December, 1916, at a cost of nearly seventy thousand dollars, and was occupied at the opening of the winter term in January, 1917. It contains rooms for two hundred and thirty-five young men. Each of the two large wings contains a suite for the use of a professor and his family. The building is in every way satisfactory, and is one of the best college dormitories in the South.

PEARSONS HALL.—No benefaction of recent years has proven more immediately serviceable than the gift of twenty thousand dollars made in 1908 by the late Dr. D. K. Pearsons, of Chicago. The new building named in his honor provides additional dormitory facilities for young women, and quarters for the large Cooperative Boarding Club. The first story contains a dining-hall, with a seating capacity of five hundred, the kitchen, offices, and waiting-rooms. The second story contains parlors, halls for the young women's literary societies, and rooms for thirty-four occupants. The third story was added during the vacation months of 1912, increasing the capacity of the dormitory so that fifty additional young women may secure rooms. This story was a gift of the late Louis H. Severance, Esq., of Cleveland, Ohio, "an admirer of Dr. Pearsons, who esteemed it a privilege to put this crowning story upon his building."

THE SWIMMING POOL.—In the original plans of Bartlett Hall, as secured by Kin Takahashi, there was provision made for the building of a swimming pool beneath the gymnasium. Lack of funds prevented the construction of the pool. In April, 1914, the Y. M. C. A. cabinet led in a movement, which rallied around it the entire student body, looking to the construction of the proposed pool. This movement was continued in "Swimming Pool Week," November 1 to 7, 1914, when the enthusiastic efforts of the students completed the raising of fifteen hundred dollars in cash toward the cost of the pool. The college authorities then undertook the building of the pool. It was opened for use at the opening of the fall term, 1915. The pool occupies a separate building fifty-eight by one hundred and ten feet. The pool itself is twenty-five by seventy-five feet in dimensions. All the appointments of the building are those approved by the best architects. The pool is a means of health and of useful sport to the students.

THE CLASS OF '16 FOUNTAIN.—In the spring of 1916 the graduating class of the College, by its own labor, constructed the Class of '16 Fountain, and presented it to the College during Commencement Week. The fountain, built of reinforced concrete and trimmed with Tennessee marble, is located on one of the principal walks, between Anderson and Fayer-weather Halls. The College is grateful to the Class of '16 for this token of their affection for their Alma Mater.

"The House in the Woods," situated in a picturesque part of the spacious college campus, was built and endowed in 1917 for the use of the present College Pastor and his successors, by a life-long friend of Mrs. William P. Stevenson, as a memorial of Mrs. Stevenson's father and mother, Mr. and Mrs. William Cooper. It is a thoroughly well-built house, provided with every modern convenience, and together with its charming woodland setting, makes a most attractive and comfortable home.

The Power Plant.—Heat for all the buildings is furnished from the central power house situated on the campus. The boilers in this plant have a combined capacity of three hundred horse-power. The Webster Vacuum System of steam heating is used, and the buildings are quickly and uniformly heated. Steam from the plant is used also for cooking and for dish-washing at the Cooperative Boarding Club.

### THE LAMAR MEMORIAL LIBRARY

The Lamar Library is one of the largest college libraries in the State. The number of books now on the shelves is about twenty thousand. The library is open for the drawing of books or for the consulting of volumes in the reference alcoves for eight hours every day from Monday to Saturday. The use of the library is entirely free to students of all departments. The nucleus of a much needed endowment for the library has been secured, the fund now amounting to about $8,000. Among the gifts making up the endowment are the following:

The "M. T." Fund, 1900, given by a friend........................ $500
The Helen Gould Fund, 1900, by Mrs. Helen Gould Shepard, New York....................................................... 500
The Willard Fund, 1900, by the Misses Willard, Auburn, N. Y..... 200
The Hollenback Fund, 1901, by J. W. Hollenback, Esq., Wilkes-barre, Pa................................................... 500
The Solomon Bogart Fund, 1908, by Miss Martha M. Bogart, Philadelphia, Tenn............................................... 200
The Nina Cunningham Fund, 1909, by the sons of the late Major Ben Cunningham, Treasurer of the College, in memory of their sister, Miss Nina Cunningham, '91........................... 500
The John M. Alexander English Literature Fund, 1909, by Rev. John M. Alexander, '87, and wife, Maryville....................... 500
The Charles T. Cates, Jr., Fund, 1909, by Hon. C. T. Cates, Jr., '81, former Attorney-General of the State of Tennessee........... 300
The Rev. S. B. West Fund, 1909-1912, by the late Mrs. S. B. West, Concord, Tenn................................................. 100

The McTeer Fund, 1909, by J. C. McTeer, '07..................... $100
The Brown Fund, 1910, by Hon. T. N. Brown, '77................. 100
The Chilhowee Club Fund, 1910, by the Chilhowee Club, Maryville. 100
The Class of 1891 Fund, 1910, by five members of the class........ 232
The George Glenn Cooper Fund, 1910-1917, by the parents, brother,
    and sister of the late George Glenn Cooper.................... 450
The Faculty Fund, 1910, by members of the Faculty............... 1,000
The French Fund, 1910, by Mr. and Mrs. C. T. French, '06........ 100
The Gamble Fund, 1910, by Hon. M. H. Gamble, '05, Hon. Andrew
    Gamble, and A. M. Gamble, M.D., Maryville.................. 250
The Hooke Fund, 1910-1917, by Rev. R. H. Hooke, '74............ 120
The Litterer Fund, 1910, by C. C. Litterer, '99.................... 50
The Lowry Fund, 1910, by Rev. G. H. Lowry, '94................. 100
The Tracy Fund, 1910, by J. E. Tracy, Esq., '01.................. 75
The Jackson Fund, 1913, by C. O. Jackson, Maryville............. 100
The Philadelphia Fund, 1909-1916, by a Friend, Philadelphia, Pa... 375
The Robert Pierce Walker Fund, 1915, by Mrs. Amanda A. Don-
    aldson...................................................... 30
The Henry Fund, 1917, by Rev. S. E. Henry, '88.................. 100
The Class of 1909 Fund........................................ 505
The Class of 1910 Fund........................................ 380
The Class of 1911 Fund........................................ 195
The Class of 1912 Fund........................................ 126
The Class of 1913 Fund........................................ 89

## LOAN LIBRARIES

**James R. Hills Library.**—In 1888 Miss Sarah B. Hills, of New York, contributed a fund of six hundred dollars for the establishment of a Loan Library, in order that students unable to purchase the necessary text-books might have the privilege of renting them at a nominal rate. By judicious management the income from this fund has grown until now the privileges of this library are open to all students, and all the regular text-books used in the institution may be either rented or purchased, as the student prefers. An additional gift of five hundred dollars from the same donor in 1908 made it possible to provide the text-books in use in the Bible Training Department. The rental charged a term is one-fifth the retail price of each book. The income from rentals is devoted to supplying new books as they are needed. The library occupies a room in Anderson Hall, and is open every day.

**John C. Branner Library.**—Some years ago John C. Branner, Ph.D., ex-President of the Leland Stanford Junior University, gave another proof of his generosity and friendship to the College by establishing a loan library of the text-books used in the natural science departments. The books in this library are under the same regulations as are those of the Hills Library.

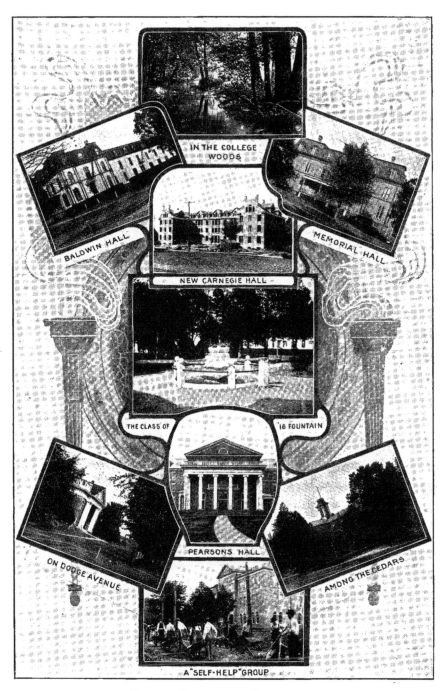

IN THE COLLEGE WOODS

BALDWIN HALL

MEMORIAL HALL

NEW CARNEGIE HALL

THE CLASS OF '16 FOUNTAIN

ON DODGE AVENUE

PEARSONS HALL

AMONG THE CEDARS

A "SELF-HELP" GROUP

CAMPUS SCENES AND DORMITORIES

**The Misses Willard Library.**—Through the generosity of the Misses Willard, of Auburn, N. Y., the text-books employed in the Bible classes of the Preparatory Department are also provided for rent at a nominal charge.

## THE COOPERATIVE BOARDING CLUB

No other agency has been of greater service in enabling the College to keep the expense of its students at a minimum than has the popular and successful Cooperative Boarding Club. The actual cost of the board is determined at the end of each month. The price is fixed approximately at the beginning of each year, and is not advanced unless absolutely necessary. Every endeavor will be made to keep the price for the ensuing year from exceeding $2.25 a week, although this can not be guaranteed during the war. A deposit of $9.00 is required of each member of the Club, and settlements are thereafter made at the end of every fourth week. Because of the cost rates at which board is furnished, a member's account with the Club is reckoned from the beginning of the college month during which he enters. A considerable number of students are employed as waiters and assistants in the dining-room, thus materially reducing the cost of their board. The privileges of the Club are extended to all male students and to all young women rooming in the college dormitories. The membership of the Club has been more than five hundred this year. The Club is housed in Pearsons Hall, spoken of elsewhere.

## COLLEGE EXPENSES

It is a constant aim of the College to provide first-class college advantages to the student at the lowest possible rates, and the endowment enables it to make its charges very moderate. College bills must be paid invariably in advance. Until this condition is complied with, no one can become a member of any of the classes. In view of the very low rates, no deduction will be made for absence at the beginning or at the end of any term, and no tuition will be refunded. Students, except those entering for the first time, that register later than the third day of any term, pay a late registration fee of two dollars.

### Fall Term

TUITION: All literary courses.................................... $6.00
  * Home Economics (one course, $3.00)......................... 6.00
  Music (vocal or instrumental):
    Under head of department, 14 lessons } .................. 7.00
    Under an assistant, 20 lessons      }
    Class lessons in Rudiments of Music, Harmony, or History of
      Music....................................................... 2.50

---

* Students enrolled in literary courses are not charged any additional tuition if they take home economics courses.

5

Expression, 14 individual lessons................................ \$9.00
Class lessons ................................................ 2.50
Art, 14 three-hour lessons in oil or water-color painting........ 7.00
FEES: War-time incidental fee (payable by all students)......... 2.00
Late-registration fee (payable only by those entering later than
the third day of the term).................................... 2.00
Laboratory fee in Chemistry or Home Economics (each course). 3.00
Laboratory fee in Biology or Advanced Physics (each course).. 2.00
Laboratory fee in Agriculture or Preparatory Sciences (each
course)...................................................... 1.00
Breakage deposit for Chemistry (each course)................... 2.00
Breakage deposit for other science courses (each course)........ 1.00
Key deposit .................................................. 1.00
Piano rental (an hour a day)................................. 4.00
TEXT-BOOKS: Rented for about one-fifth retail price of the book,
average ..................................................... 1.75
ROOM RENT: (consult the detailed statement under Rooms) average. 12.00
* BOARD: In the Cooperative Boarding Club, about \$2.25 a week,
approximately ............................................... 32.00
In private families, \$4.00 to \$6.00 a week.
APPROXIMATE EXPENSES FOR THE FALL TERM: \$55.00 to \$70.00.

## Winter or Spring Term

TUITION: All literary courses................................. \$6.00
† Home Economics (one course, \$3.00)......................... 6.00
Music (vocal or instrumental):
Under head of department, 11 lessons }
Under an assistant, 15 lessons           }  ................... 5.50
Class lessons in Rudiments of Music, Harmony, or History of
Music (winter and spring terms combined)................. 3.00
Expression, 11 individual lessons............................. 7.00
Class lessons (winter and spring terms combined)........... 3.00
Art, 11 three-hour lessons in oil or water-color painting........ 5.50
FEES: War-time incidental fee (payable by all students)......... 2.00
Athletic and forensic fee (payable by all students)............. 1.00
Late-registration fee (payable only by those entering later than
the third day of the term).................................... 2.00
Laboratory fee in Chemistry (each course)..................... 2.50
Laboratory fee in Home Economics (each course)............... 3.00
Laboratory fee in Biology or Advanced Physics (each course).. 2.00
Laboratory fee in Agriculture or Preparatory Sciences (each
course)...................................................... 1.00

---

* Read THE COOPERATIVE BOARDING CLUB, page 65.
† Students enrolled in literary courses are not charged any additional tuition if they take home economics courses.

Breakage deposit for Chemistry (each course)................... $1.50
Breakage deposit for other science courses (each course)........ 1.00
Key deposit .................................................... 1.00
Piano rental (an hour a day).................................... 3.00
Graduation fees (payable at the opening of the spring term of
    the graduating year) :
    College Department ........................................ 5.00
    Preparatory Department .................................... 1.00
    Home Economics Department.................................. 2.50
    Music Department .......................................... 2.50
    Expression Department ..................................... 2.50
TEXT-BOOKS : Rented for about one-fifth retail price of the book,
    average for winter and spring terms combined................ 1.75
ROOM RENT : (consult the detailed statement under Rooms) average :
    Winter term ............................................... 10.00
    Spring term ............................................... 8.00
* BOARD : In the Cooperative Boarding Club, about $2.25 a week,
    for either winter or spring term, approximately............. 25.00
In private families, $4.00 to $6.00 a week.
APPROXIMATE EXPENSES FOR THE WINTER TERM : $45.00 to $60.00.
APPROXIMATE EXPENSES FOR THE SPRING TERM are about $5.00 less
than for the winter term.
APPROXIMATE EXPENSES FOR THE YEAR (THREE TERMS) :
For the student not taking science courses, music, expression, or
    art, about ................................................ 140.00
For the student taking science courses, but not music, expression,
    or art, about............................................. 150.00
For the student taking principally music, expression, or art...... 180.00

### Christmas Holidays

The rates in the foregoing tables do not include room rent or board for the vacation period between the fall and winter terms. Carnegie and Pearsons Halls are kept open, however, and a nominal maintenance charge is made of those that remain on the hill, and board is furnished at the most reasonable rates possible. The cost to the student that remains at the College during the Christmas holidays has not as yet exceeded $2.50 for room rent, with light and heat, and $7.00 for board, for the entire vacation period.

### Rooms

Every prospective student desiring to room in a dormitory must make a two-dollar deposit with the Registrar in order to secure a reservation. The Registrar will send the applicant a deposit receipt, which, upon presentation by the student when he enters college, will be accepted by the

---

* Read THE COOPERATIVE BOARDING CLUB, page 65.

Treasurer for credit on the room rent to the amount and for the term specified thereon. The room, however, will not be held beyond the opening day unless the room rent is paid for the term in advance. The deposit receipt is not negotiable, and the deposit will be forfeited if the student does not enter college.

All the dormitories are heated with steam and lighted with electricity, and are fully supplied with wardrobes, baths, and toilets. All the rooms contain the following articles of furniture: individual iron bedsteads, springs, mattresses, tables with built-in bookcases, chairs, and, for young women, dressers; for young men, chiffoniers. The student will provide bedding and any other necessity not here specified. Two students occupy one room. According to location the rates for each student are as follows:

|  | Fall Term | Winter Term | Spring Term |
|---|---|---|---|
| MEMORIAL HALL (men) | $11.00 to $13.00 | $9.00 to $11.00 | $7.00 to $9.00 |
| CARNEGIE HALL (men) | 10.00 to 17.00 | 8.00 to 14.00 | 6.00 to 10.00 |
| BALDWIN HALL (women) | 9.00 to 14.00 | 7.00 to 11.00 | 5.00 to 8.00 |
| PEARSONS HALL (women) | 13.00 to 16.00 | 11.00 to 13.00 | 7.00 to 9.00 |

### ROOMS IN TOWN

Young men can find comfortable furnished rooms in private residences in convenient parts of town at the following rates by the month for each student:

Rooms furnished and cared for, without fuel or light...... $2.50 to $4.00
Rooms furnished and cared for, with light and heat....... 3.00 to 5.00

### Laundry

In the Cooperative Laundry (young women doing their own
work).................................................. $0.30 a month
In town by private laundresses..................... $0.35 to $0.75 a week

## STUDENTS' ORGANIZATIONS

**Literary Societies.**—Four literary societies are conducted by the students, and are of the greatest benefit to those who avail themselves of the advantages they offer. The ATHENIAN, organized in 1868, and the ALPHA SIGMA, organized in 1882, are composed of young men. Each society is divided into a "senior section" and a "junior section," the latter being composed of students in the Preparatory Department. Their halls, four in number, are on the third floor of Anderson Hall. The BAINONIAN, organized in 1875, and the THETA EPSILON, organized in 1894, are conducted by the young women. They have neatly furnished halls in Pearsons Hall. The societies meet every Saturday evening to engage in debates and other literary exercises. Each society gives annually a public midwinter entertainment.

**The Y. M. C. A. and Y. W. C. A.**—The Y. M. C. A., established in 1877, has become one of the strongest organizations of its kind in the South. The weekly devotional meetings are held on Sabbath afternoon in the auditorium of Bartlett Hall. The officers of the Association are as follows: President, Horace Dawson; Vice President, Deck C. Williams; Secretary, William B. Holmes; Treasurer, David H. Briggs; Cabinet, Robert L. Taylor, Homer G. Weisbecker, Robert W. Adams, Robert M. Bartlett, and Harold E. Smith.

The Advisory Committee of the Y. M. C. A., composed of representatives of the Faculty and of the student body, directs the general policies of the Association. It consists of the following members: Class of 1918: Dean Barnes, Chairman, President Wilson, and Professor Bassett; Class of 1919: Professor Gillingham, Roy R. Anderson, and Jason G. Purdy; Class of 1920: Treasurer Proffitt, Major Will A. McTeer, and Ralph E. Smith.

The Y. W. C. A. was established in 1884, and has become one of the most wholesome influences in the religious life of the College. The weekly devotional meetings are held on Sabbath afternoons in the association room, in the basement of Voorhees Chapel. The Association has a small but valuable library, known as the Florence McManigal Memorial Library. It was contributed by Rev. J. Oscar Boyd, Ph.D., and wife, of Paterson, N. J., as a memorial to their sister, Miss McManigal, '08, who was an instructor in the College and who died in 1909. The officers of the Association are as follows: President, George Ella Simpson; Vice President, Mary E. Heard; Secretary, Jessie A. Creswell; Treasurer, Edith W. Moore; Editor, Helen Lewis; Cabinet, D. Grace Bailey, Ashton B Clayton, Winston C. Newton, Idella Hemphill, Della Carpenter, Agnes I. Dolvin, Mamie E. Pleasants, and Eleanor D. Moseley.

**The Athletic Association.**—This organization is maintained by the student body for the purpose of regulating athletics and caring for athletic equipment. The Board of Athletic Control, composed of representatives of the Faculty, the students, and former students, meets at stated intervals and exercises oversight over all the athletic events of the College. Upon the recommendation of this Board, the Directors of the College have voted an athletic and forensic fee of one dollar a term payable by all students, and entitling every student to admission to all athletic and forensic events. The football and baseball fields, the tennis courts, the track, and the basketball court are open to any student desiring to enter these forms of sport.

The members of the Board of Athletic Control, whose officers are also the officers of the Athletic Association, are as follows: Director of Athletics and Head Coach, Edgar O. Brown; Chairman, Alton D. Bryson; Secretary, John K. Witherspoon; Treasurer and Official Buyer, Treasurer Proffitt; Faculty Representatives, President Wilson and Professors Knapp and Ellis; Student Representatives, Glen A. Lloyd, F. Gaston Cooper,

Robert B. Clemens, Eleanor D. Moseley, and J. Maude Pardue; Town Representatives, John A. McCulloch, M.D., and C. Francis Kelly.

The officers of the athletic teams are as follows: Managers: Football, Alton D. Bryson; Basketball, John K. Witherspoon; Women's Basketball, Ethel L. Burchfiel; Baseball, Frank H. Scruggs; Track, George B. Callahan; Tennis, Homer G. Weisbecker. Captains: Football, Robert B. Clemens; Basketball, D. Parks Eagleton; Women's Basketball, Beatrice I. Marshall; Baseball, Horace Dawson.

**The Ministerial Association,** organized in 1900, is composed of the candidates for the Christian ministry that are in attendance upon the College. It has for its object the enlistment of its members in various forms of active Christian work, and the discussion of themes relating to the work of the ministry. Its officers are: President, Cedric V. Miller; Vice President, Onessus H. Logan; Secretary and Treasurer, George D. Howell; Superintendent of Mission Work, William E. McCurry.

**The Student Volunteer Band.**—The College has from its earliest history been identified with foreign missions, and has sent out fifty-two missionaries into fourteen foreign countries. Since 1894 the students have maintained a Student Volunteer Band, composed of those who are pledged to enter some foreign field, if the way be open. The Band meets weekly to study missionary fields and conditions. The officers for the present year are as follows: President, Mary Miles; Vice President, Howard D. McGrath; Secretary and Treasurer, Maude C. Hite; Editor, Ernest E. Loft.

**The Intercollegiate Prohibition Association.**—Interest and participation in the prohibition movement have been characteristic of the Faculty and students of the College from its foundation. The object of this association is to obtain and circulate information regarding the prohibition movement throughout the United States, to deepen interest therein, and to train participants in intercollegiate contests conducted under the management of the larger Association, of which the local organization is a part. The officers are: President, George A. Harris; Vice President, D. Grace Bailey; Secretary and Treasurer, Maude C. Hite; Editor, Carrie B. Sheddan.

**The Law Club.**—The young men that are studying with a view to entering the profession of law maintain an organization known as the Law Club. Their purpose is to familiarize themselves with the features of their contemplated life work, and to develop high moral standards and ideals in connection with their profession. The officers of the club are: President, Jason B. Deyton; Vice President, Robert W. Adams; Secretary and Treasurer, Tien Ze Chang; Program Secretary, Oscar Stanton.

**The Equal Suffrage League.**—The young women interested in the extension of the franchise have formed an organization for the purpose of studying the progress of the equal suffrage movement and the phases of the political and moral welfare of the nation that are particularly affected thereby, and also of cultivating among college students a wider, sympathetic interest in the movement. The league is actively cooperating with the Red Cross in the making of bandages, sweaters, mufflers, wristlets, and the like. It has also recently adopted a French orphan boy who was born just after the outbreak of the war and whose father has been killed in battle. The officers of the league are: President, Elizabeth A. Henry; Vice President, Mattie M. Fisher; Secretary, J. Maude Pardue; Treasurer, Claudia Bogart.

**The Pre-medical Club.**—Students preparing for the practice of medicine, including both those in the regular classes and those taking the special pre-medical course, have organized with a view to a better understanding of the problems and interests of the medical profession. The officers are: President, Harold E. Smith; Vice President, N. Arthur Podesta; Secretary and Treasurer, Jarvis M. Cotton; Editor, C. Yeatman Latimer.

### ALUMNI ASSOCIATION

This Association was formed in 1871. It holds its annual meeting on Commencement Day, when a banquet is given under the auspices of the Faculty of the College and the local alumni. The officers for 1917-1918 are as follows: President, William T. Bartlett, '01; Vice President, George M. Adams, '16; Secretary, Samuel T. Wilson, '78; Executive Committee, Charles W. Henry, '01, Nellie C. Pickens, '13, Erma M. Hall, '14, Aletha M. Armstrong, '16, and David W. Proffitt, '16; Manager of the Alumni and Undergraduate Scholarship Fund, Henry J. Bassett, '04.

### ROLL OF HONOR

More than three hundred of the male graduates and undergraduates of the College are known to have enlisted for the war in some branch of national military service. An honor roll of the names of these men was begun early in 1917 and is still being added to. A large Service Flag, eight by sixteen feet, has been raised in the college chapel, with stars for all those whose names have been secured. Information regarding the whereabouts and welfare of those on the honor roll, or the name of any one that should be added, will be heartily welcomed, and should be sent to the Registrar.

### THE Y. M. C. A. LYCEUM COURSE

For several years the Y. M. C. A. has conducted for the student body and the public a course of lectures and entertainments. The course usually consists of five numbers, one or two of which are popular lectures and the rest musical, elocutionary, or dramatic entertainments. The course is provided at small cost to the student, tickets for the entire series costing usually a dollar and a half.

## FORENSIC CONTESTS AND PRIZES

For several years debating contests have been held with Tusculum College, Tennessee, in which each institution debates the other on the same date. During a part of the time these contests were triangular, Carson and Newman College, Tennessee, being the third member. These contests are held during the spring term.

A debate with Emory and Henry College, Virginia, the contest being held at Maryville; and a dual debate between the preparatory departments of Maryville College and Lincoln Memorial University, Tennessee, were arranged for 1917-1918.

The Athenian and Alpha Sigma Literary Societies hold public contests in oratory and debate. These contests are sometimes intersociety and sometimes intrasociety, and are usually for medals offered by the societies or an alumnus.

The Board of Temperance of the Presbyterian Church, U. S. A., offers annually prizes amounting to twenty-five dollars for orations on phases of the prohibition problem. Public contests are held during the winter or spring term, and are open to any college student. The interstate contest of the Intercollegiate Prohibition Association was held at Maryville in 1917-1918.

THE WILLIAM H. BATES ORATORICAL PRIZE FOUNDATION.—Rev. William Henry Bates, D.D., of Greeley, Colorado, during the past year contributed to the College the sum of seven hundred and fifty dollars to form a fund, the annual income of which shall be used to provide a prize in oratory to be contested for by the members of the Senior Class. The first contest will take place next year, and will be conducted in accordance with rules prepared by the Faculty after conference with the donor of the fund.

A local contest in oratory under the auspices of the Intercollegiate Peace Association is held annually, in which any college student may participate. The winner in this contest becomes eligible to enter the state contest. No permanent prize for this contest has as yet been contributed, but a prize amounting to ten dollars has generally been secured for the winning contestant.

## PHYSICAL CULTURE

Classes are conducted by the physical directors daily, and all students, except members of the Junior and Senior Classes, local students in the Preparatory Department, and cadets taking military training, are required to avail themselves of the privilege afforded, unless excused by reason of physical disability, or of being members of regular athletic teams. Excuses for any other reason must be approved by the faculty before being accepted. A physical examination is required annually of every student. The classes for the young men and the young women meet in their respective gymnasiums and under the direction of their respective physical directors. The work offered is carefully graded and adjusted to the needs of the various classes. Credit equivalent to one recitation hour is given for the satisfactory completion of each two hours' work during the term. Every young woman should bring a gymnasium suit, preferably consisting of a white or blue middy and blue bloomers, and gymnasium or tennis shoes. Every young man should bring a regulation white gymnasium suit, consisting of sleeveless shirt, running pants, support, and gymnasium or tennis shoes.

The swimming pool is open three days each week for the young men and on the alternating three days for the young women. Careful supervision of the pool is given at all times, and no one is permitted in the pool except when a physical director is present. The pool is kept in the best sanitary condition. Shower baths in a separate room are provided and required to be used before a person is permitted to enter the pool.

## MILITARY TRAINING

In harmony with the spirit of patriotic service prevailing among educational institutions generally, the College has provided for military drill. Two drills a week are conducted by student officers under the supervision of the Commandant, who is an officer in the United States National Guard. The opportunity for instruction and drill in infantry tactics is available to all students, and young men who are of military age are especially urged to join the battalion. The cadets are excused from taking other physical training and are given physical culture credit for their company and battalion drills. During the past year the Commandant also conducted two courses in military tactics especially for those intending to enlist in the Army. Fifty-five men took this special training.

Cadets wear a khaki uniform, which makes a serviceable school suit and which may be purchased through the College at a reasonable price. The uniforms worn during the past year, for blouse, breeches, leggings, and hat, averaged ten dollars. Students intending to take the military drill should come prepared to purchase a uniform.

## MEDICAL ATTENTION

The Ralph Max Lamar Memorial Hospital, spoken of elsewhere, is available for all students. A nurse looks after the general health of the students, and nurses all cases that require her attention. In cases of slight illness no charge is made for nursing, but the patient pays $4.00 a week for the use of the ward, and for board and laundry. In cases of serious illness demanding more than ordinary time and attention, a nominal charge is also made for the nursing. On Tuesday, Thursday, and Friday of each week free medical consultation and prescription by approved physicians are provided at the hospital for out-of-town students. Any other medical attention, however, that may be required must be paid for by the student.

These privileges have been responded to with marked appreciation by the student body, and the medical attention thus afforded has been of great service in the prevention and checking of serious illness.

## ADMINISTRATIVE RULES

ABSENCE FROM THE COLLEGE.—Students are not allowed to absent themselves from the College without permission from the Faculty.

ABSENCE FROM REQUIRED DUTY.—See rule regarding demerits and unexcused absences.

CHANGES OF COURSE.—All changes of studies must be made within two weeks after matriculation. Thereafter, all changes for students in the Preparatory Department shall be made by order of the Principal of the department, and all changes in the College Department by permission of the Faculty, and in all cases after consultation with the instructors concerned. Every change of course made after two weeks from date of matriculation involves a fee of fifty cents, unless this fee is remitted by special vote of the Faculty.

DEMERITS AND UNEXCUSED ABSENCES.—Demerits and unexcused absences are recorded separately. If a student accrues ten demerits or ten unexcused absences within any one term, he is suspended for at least the remainder of that term. Unexcused absences reduce grades in proportion to the time of absence. Excused absences also reduce grades in proportion to the time of absence, unless the work is made up. This applies to all absences due to late registration.

DISMISSAL FROM COLLEGE.—Students are dismissed, also, whenever in the opinion of the Faculty they are pursuing a course of conduct detrimental to themselves and to the College. The Faculty are the sole judges of the advisability of such dismissal. Maryville College is a private institution, and reserves the right to dismiss a student whenever the authorities of the College may elect. An institution which is affording such extensive opportunities and advantages to its students in return for fees not so large as the incidental fees of most institutions, can not allow those to remain in attendance who fail to perform their college work, or who injure college property, disturb college order, or by acts of insubordination or immorality hurt the good name of the College and add unnecessary burdens to the authorities of the institution. The College desires no such students, and rids itself of them when they appear.

DISORDER.—Promoting or participating in class clashes or fights, and hazing or other interference with individual liberty or class functions on the part of individuals or classes, are prohibited. Applicants for admission are referred to the paragraphs on Admission to the College, or Admission to the Preparatory Department.

ENTERTAINMENTS.—To avoid interference with the regular work of the College, students must secure special permission before engaging in any entertainment outside the College.

EXAMINATIONS.—A student absent from any examination without an approved excuse will be marked "zero" on that examination, and will receive no credit for his term's work. Any student failing to be present at term examinations shall be required to take all omitted examinations before being allowed to enter classes on his return to the College. A fee of one dollar will be charged for any examination given at any other time than that set for the regular examinations.

FORFEITURE OF AID.—Any student receiving financial aid from the College, in the form of scholarships, loans, or opportunities for work, will forfeit such aid if he becomes an object of college discipline.

LATE REGISTRATION.—Students, except those entering for the first time, that register later than the third day of any term, pay an additional fee of two dollars. Absence due to late registration reduces grades in proportion to the time of absence, unless the work is made up.

RELIGIOUS SERVICES.—Prayers are attended in the college chapel in the morning, with the reading of the Scripture and with singing. Every student is required to attend public worship on the Sabbath, and to connect himself with a Sabbath-school class in some one of the churches in town, and to make a written honor report each week to his chapel monitor.

ROOMING IN TOWN.—Students are not permitted to room or to board at hotels or other places disapproved by the Faculty. Young women from out of town are not permitted to room or board off the college grounds, except with relatives.

SABBATH.—Students are not allowed to patronize the Sunday trains or to visit the railway stations on the Sabbath. No student will be received on the Sabbath. Sunday visits are disapproved.

SECRET SOCIETIES.—No secret socity will be allowed among the students, and no organization will be permitted that has not been approved by the Faculty.

STANDING.—A uniform system of grading is employed, upon the results of which depends the promotion from one class to another. The Faculty meets each week of the college year, and receives reports of the work done in all departments and of the delinquencies of individual students. A record is made of the standing of each student, which is sent to his parents or guardians at the end of each term. In order to be classified in any given year in the College Department a student shall not be conditioned in more than three studies.

TOBACCO.—The use of tobacco on the college grounds and in the college buildings is forbidden, and no student addicted to its use will be allowed to room upon the college premises. One violation of this rule will be deemed sufficient to exclude a student from the college dormitories.

VACCINATION.—Vaccination is required of those students who have not recently been vaccinated.

## SELF-HELP

The College offers opportunities of self-help to a large number of deserving young men and young women. About three hundred annually avail themselves of such opportunities. The work offered includes manual labor on the grounds, janitor service in the various buildings, dining-room and kitchen service at the Cooperative Boarding Club, office work, and work as assistants in laboratories or libraries. These forms of employment are paid for at a rate varying according to the degree of skill and responsibility involved. Indoor work is allotted usually to students that have previously given proof of their ability and worth. Positions of exceptional responsibility, such as janitor service and work as assistants, are granted for a year in advance, the assignment being made at the close of the spring term. Assistants in any department are elected by the Faculty upon the recommendation of the head of the department.

Application for work of any kind must be made in writing and addressed to the Faculty. The acceptance of an opportunity of self-help involves especial obligation to diligence, loyalty, and the faithful discharge of duty. A student that fails to do satisfactory work or becomes an object of discipline by the Faculty will forfeit all such opportunities.

## SCHOLARSHIP FUNDS

The Craighead Fund, 1886, contributed by Rev. James G. Craighead, D.D., of Washington, D. C., for candidates for the ministry... $1,500

The Carson Adams Fund, 1887, by Rev. Carson W. Adams, D.D., of New York, for tuition help... 6,300

The George Henry Bradley Scholarship, 1889, by Mrs. Jane Loomis Bradley, of Auburn, N. Y., in memory of her only son... 1,000

The Willard Scholarship, 1898, by the Misses Willard, of Auburn, New York ... 1,000

The Students' Self-help Loan Fund, 1903, 1908, and 1912, by Rev. Nathan Bachman, D.D., of Sweetwater, Tenn., for loans to upper classmen ... 2,000

The Clement Ernest Wilson Scholarship, 1904, by the late Mrs. Mary A. Wilson, of Maryville, in memory of her son... 1,000

The Alumni and Undergraduate Scholarship Fund, begun 1904, by the Alumni Association and former students. A bequest of $500 was made to the fund by the late Mrs. M. A. Wilson, of Maryville ... 2,703

The Angier Self-help Work and Loan Fund, 1907-1911, by Mr. Albert E. Angier, of Boston, Mass., to provide opportunities of work and loans for young men.............................. $5,000

The Margaret E. Henry Scholarship, 1907, established through the efforts of Mr. Jasper E. Corning, of New York.............. 1,000

The Arta Hope Scholarship, 1907, by Miss Arta Hope, of Robinson, Ill...................................................... 1,000

The Hugh O'Neill, Jr., Scholarship, 1908, by Mrs. Hugh O'Neill, of New York, in memory of her son......................... 1,000

The Alexander Caldwell Memorial Fund, 1908, by Mr. G. A. Moody, of Jefferson City, Tenn., the income to be loaned.............. 1,000

The D. Stuart Dodge Scholarship, 1908, by Rev. D. Stuart Dodge, D.D., of New York City, preferably to aid graduates of the Farm School of North Carolina.............................. 1,500

The Julia M. Turner Missionary Scholarship Fund, 1908, by Mrs. Julia M. Turner, to aid the children of foreign missionaries or those preparing for the foreign field......................... 5,000

The William J. McCahan, Sr., Fund, 1908, by Mr. William J. McCahan, Sr., of Philadelphia, Pa., for tuition help.............. 5,000

The W. A. E. Campbell Foreign Missionary Fund, 1909, by Rev. W. A. E. Campbell, of Hanna City, Ill., to aid a young woman preparing for foreign missionary work........................ 700

The Charles Francis Darlington, Jr., Scholarship, 1909, by Mrs. Letitia Craig Darlington, of New York, in honor of her son... 1,000

The Hoover Self-help Fund, 1909, by Dr. W. A. Hoover, of Gibson City, Ill., to provide opportunities of work for young men..... 500

The Isaac Anderson Scholarship, 1909 and 1916, by James A. and Howard Anderson, of Knoxville, Tenn., in memory of their great-uncle, Rev. Isaac Anderson, D.D., the founder of Maryville College ...................................................... 2,000

The John H. Converse Scholarship, 1909, by Mr. John H. Converse, of Philadelphia, Pa., for candidates for the ministry and other Christian service ......................................... 5,000

The Chattanooga Self-help Fund, 1910, by Rev. E. A. Elmore, D.D., and other citizens of Chattanooga, Tenn., to provide opportunities of work for students.................................. 500

The Rena Sturtevant Memorial Scholarship, 1910, by Miss Anna St. John, of New York..................................... 1,000

The Nathaniel Tooker Scholarship, 1910, by Nathaniel Tooker, Esq., East Orange, N. J........................................... 1,000

The James R. Hills Memorial Self-help Work Fund, 1911, by Miss Sarah B. Hills, of New York, to provide work for students.... 1,000

The Mrs. Elizabeth Hyde Mead Memorial Scholarship, 1911, by the Abbot Collegiate Association of New York.................... 1,000

The G. S. W. Crawford Self-help Fund, 1912, by friends of the late
Professor Crawford, to provide work for students............. $1,000
The Elizabeth Belcher Bullard Memorial Scholarship, 1912, "given
in memory of a great friendship" by Mrs. Elizabeth C. Barney
Buel, of East Meadows, Litchfield, Conn., through the Mary
Floyd Tallmadge Chapter of the D. A. R................... 1,000
The Elizabeth Hillman Memorial Scholarship, 1912 and 1914, by Mrs.
John Hartwell Hillman, of Pittsburgh, Pa., through the Pitts-
burgh Chapter of the D. A. R., "in perpetuity for mountain girls
in Maryville College," $2,000; additional, 1918, by Miss Sara F.
Hillman, of Pittsburgh, Pa., for the paying of young women as
laboratory assistants in science departments, $2,500........... 4,500
The Robert A. Tedford Scholarship, 1913, "given by his wife, Emma
Patton Tedford, as a memorial to her husband".............. 1,000
The Major Ben and Jane A. Cunningham Fund, 1914, by Edwin S.,
Campbell S., Clay, and Ben Cunningham, to assist worthy and
needy students, preferably from Blount County, Tennessee..... 1,045
The Mary Harwood Memorial Scholarship, 1915, by the Stamford,
Conn., Chapter of the D. A. R., "to aid worthy students"...... 1,000
The Harriet Van Auken Craighead Memorial Scholarship, 1916, by
Miss Alice W. Craighead, of Washington, D. C., to aid prefer-
ably young women from the Southern Appalachians, preparing
to be teachers................................................ 1,500
The Elizabeth B. Camm Cornell Scholarship, 1916, bequest of the
late Elizabeth B. Camm Cornell, of Newtown, Pa............ 1,000
The Rachel Dornan Scholarship, 1916, bequest of the late Rachel
Dornan, of New York........................................ 1,000
The Margaret E. Henry Loan Fund, 1916, by Dr. S. Elizabeth Winter, of Philadelphia, Pa..................................... 1,000
The Margaret E. Henry Scholarship, 1916, by A Friend, of Over-
brook, Pa................................................... 1,000
The Martha A. Lamar Scholarship, 1916, by Mrs. Martha A. Lamar,
of Maryville, preferably to aid "students that are kinsmen of
mine" ...................................................... 1,000
The John and Susan M'Galliard Memorial Scholarship and Self-
help Work Fund, 1917, by Miss Fannie J. M'Galliard, of Bridge-
ton, N. J................................................... 1,000
The Charles W. Black Scholarship Fund, 1917, by Mr. Charles W.
Black, of Malvern, Iowa.................................... 1,000

## THE MARGARET E. HENRY MEMORIAL FUND

During the last thirteen years of her connection with the College,
Miss Margaret E. Henry, as scholarship secretary and field representa-

tive, secured contributions to current and permanent funds amounting to $122,693.00, besides raising up a host of friends interested in the students and work of Maryville College. Immediately following Miss Henry's death on July 7, 1916, suggestions came from some of these friends that a permanent memorial fund of one hundred thousand dollars be solicited to carry on, in part, the altruistic service to which she had devoted her life. Thus far the memorial fund amounts to $18,824.00, made up of the following scholarship and work funds:

The Julia Crouse Houser Fund, Akron, O., 1916.................. $1,000
The Mary R. Tooker Fund, East Orange, N. J., 1916............. 1,000
The Gertrude Tooker Fund, East Orange, N. J., 1916............ 1,000
The Dr. S. Elizabeth Winter Fund, Philadelphia, Pa., 1916....... 5,000
The Arthur B. Emmons Fund, Newport, R. I., 1916.............. 1,000
The Archibald Hilton Bull, Jr., Memorial Fund, 1916, by Mr. and
    Mrs. A. H. Bull, Elizabeth, N. J........................... 1,000
The Julia Spencer Whittemore Memorial Fund, 1916, by Mrs. Harris
    Whittemore, Naugatuck, Conn........................... 1,000
The James Stuart Dickson Memorial Fund, 1916, by Rev. and Mrs.
    Reid S. Dickson, Lewistown, Pa........................... 1,000
A friend in New York City, 1916................................ 500
The Dr. George W. Holmes Memorial Fund, 1916, by Mrs. George
    W. Holmes, Boonton, N. J................................ 1,000
The Eleanor G. Park Fund, Allegheny, Pa., 1917................. 2,000
The Thomas Hammond Foulds Memorial Fund, 1917, by Dr. Thomas
    H. Foulds, Glens Falls, N. Y.............................. 1,000
Received in contributions of less than $500..................... 2,324

## COLLEGE PUBLICATIONS

The official publication of the College is THE MARYVILLE COLLEGE BULLETIN. It is issued four times a year, and is sent free to any who apply for it. The May number of each year is the annual catalog. THE HIGHLAND ECHO is issued weekly by the students, the editorial staff consisting of representatives of the four literary societies, the Christian Associations, the Athletic Association, and the Alumni Association. THE CHILHOWEAN is ordinarily issued annually by the Junior Class. It is the yearbook of the student body, containing a summarized record of the year's work in all the departments and organizations of the College, and is an attractive souvenir. THE MARYVILLE HANDBOOK is ordinarily issued annually by the Christian Associations. It is intended to present the work of the Associations to new students, and also to assist them in adjusting themselves to their new environment. The publication of THE CHILHOWEAN and THE HANDBOOK has been temporarily discontinued on account of the war.

## A CENTURY OF MARYVILLE COLLEGE

At the request of The Directors of Maryville College, President Wilson, in 1916, gathered into a volume entitled "A Century of Maryville College — A Story of Altruism," the romantic story of the institution from its inception to the present time. "It was the writer's good fortune to be at first a student and then a colleague of Professor Lamar, who in turn was a student and then a colleague of Dr. Anderson; and so the writer received almost at first hand the story of Maryville, extending from the beginning down to the time when he himself entered the faculty of the College." The first edition has already had wide distribution. The Registrar will mail the book, postpaid, upon the receipt of one dollar the copy.

## THE CENTENNIAL FORWARD FUND OF $325,000

Maryville College will complete its first century of service on Commencement Day, 1919. A program of celebration appropriate to the occasion has been planned, and a large "home coming" of Maryville's sons and daughters is anticipated.

The closing years of this notable first century of the College are crowded, on the one hand, with embarrassing riches of clientage and opportunity, and, on the other hand, with an embarrassing lack of endowment and income. Since the College sternly and religiously limits the amount of its expenditures to the size of its income, it follows that such needs as are not provided for by the revenues must go unmet. The South is developing with marvelous rapidity. Country life is becoming more attractive than heretofore; and the Southern Appalachian field is calling for the best that can be done in the line of education.

In order to enable the institution to enter upon the second century somewhat more adequately equipped to meet its opportunities and to perform its obligations, the Directors of the College decided, in 1916, that a special Centennial Forward Fund should be sought, which, it is hoped, will, when completed, amount to three hundred and twenty-five thousand dollars. All contributions to permanent endowment funds and to building and equipment funds made up to June, 1919, will be credited toward this fund.

Some of the most urgent needs of the College that would be provided for by the securing of this Centennial Fund are the following: (1) The increase of the now inadequate salaries of the teaching force to a more nearly living-wage standard. At present the college faculty receive salaries considerably below what they would receive in the high schools throughout the greater part of our country; while the preparatory teachers receive much smaller salaries than they would command in regular high-school work. It is not right that these faithful and efficient men and women, whose moral purpose and college loyalty hold them in their positions of instruction at Maryville, should be so poorly paid that anxiety and self-sacrifice must be their lot. Moreover, as the cost of living advances, it is becoming increasingly difficult for the College, with its low salaries, to secure the services of suitable and competent additional professors as they are needed. The high standards of the institution as well as justice to the people who teach are both imperiled by the inadequate salaries that are now paid. The sum that is sought for the increase of the salaries of the teaching force is $75,000. The annual income of this amount would be $4,500. (2) Endowment for a manual training department, $25,000. Too long has this important and most practical department been delayed. (3) Endowment for the agricultural department, $25,000. The clientage of Maryville, the rapid and cheering development of rural life in the South, the need that present-day public-school teachers have of training in agriculture, and the trend of the times all demand this new department. Nothing in recent years has aroused so many favorable comments as has the announcement of the intention of the College to establish such a department. (4) A hospital endowment to provide the salary of the nurse, $10,000. The hospital is proving invaluable, and the nurse is necessary, and the students are unable to pay for one. Thus far, $1,156 has been paid in on this fund. (5) Additional endowment for the library, the general laboratory and work-shop of all departments of the College, $15,000. The present endowment is about eight thousand dollars. (6) Endowment to pay the administrative expenses of the Cooperative Boarding Club so as to keep the cost of board at a minimum, $15,000. Thousands of students have been enabled to attend college because of this remarkable club. This year more than five hundred students have been members of the Club. (7) Stack-room and reading-room for the Library, $10,000. This addition is absolutely necessary for the proper utilizing of the present Library. What is, however, urgently needed is a new and complete library building, costing $75,000. (8) A new central recitation building, $75,000. It can not be long deferred. All available recitation space is utilized, and yet the work is sorely cramped. The only recitation buildings are the old original Anderson Hall and the Fayerweather Science Hall. (9) Another dormitory for young women, at least, $50,000. Both dormitories for the young women are crowded, and the overflow has to be provided for. (10) Equipment of the manual training and agricultural departments, $10,000. (11) For streets, walks, and other improvements of the campus, $10,000. The grounds have been reluctantly left unimproved through lack of funds. (12) To install a pipe organ in the chapel, $5,000.

All these great needs can be met with three hundred and twenty-five thousand dollars. And the College earnestly asks the friends of education to help it secure this amount by Centennial Commencement Day, 1919, that it may begin the new century with ability commensurate with its opportunity.

All general correspondence regarding the Centennial Forward Fund should be addressed to PRESIDENT SAMUEL T. WILSON or to PROFESSOR

6

CLINTON H. GILLINGHAM; all correspondence regarding scholarships and self-help work funds, to the Chairman of the Scholarship Committee; while all correspondence regarding the agricultural department, and all contributions to the Centennial Forward Fund should be addressed to TREASURER FRED L. PROFFITT.

## THE GENERAL EDUCATION BOARD'S GRANT

At its meeting in January, 1916, the General Education Board appropriated the sum of seventy-five thousand dollars toward the above-mentioned three hundred and twenty-five thousand dollar Centennial Fund, to be paid on condition that the entire fund be secured within a specified time. Not only is this conditional appropriation a great gift in itself considered, for it is almost one-fourth of the entire amount sought, but it is also a notable tribute to the standards and work of Maryville. And this is especially true in view of the fact that this is the Board's second appropriation to Maryville, the Board having made a grant of fifty thousand dollars, in 1907, to the "Forward Fund of Two Hundred Thousand Dollars." The friends of the College are profoundly grateful to the General Education Board for these epoch-making grants made the institution in its times of need, opportunity, and crisis.

## BEQUESTS AND DEVISES

Since each State has special statutory regulations in regard to wills, it is most important that all testamentary papers be signed, witnessed, and executed according to the laws of the State in which the testator resides. In all cases, however, the legal name of the corporation must be accurately given, as in the following form:

"I give and bequeath .......... to 'THE DIRECTORS OF MARYVILLE COLLEGE,' at Maryville, Tennessee, and to their successors and assigns forever, for the uses and purposes of said College, according to the provisions of its charter."

# DEGREES AND DIPLOMAS, 1917

## DOCTOR OF DIVINITY, HONORARY
Joseph McClellan Broady

## BACHELOR OF ARTS

Frances Elizabeth Akerstrom

Dorothy Jean Carson

Herman Luther Caton

Anne Gamble Creswell

Mark Blaine Crum

Charles Edward Ensign

Robert Speer Gamon

Nellie James Garrison, *cum laude*

William Wade Haggard

Lily Canzada Henry

Mary Craig Hickey, *class orator, summa cum laude*

George Winfred Hodges

Cora Frances Hopkins

Anna Josephine Jones, *cum laude*

Chester Fred Leonard, *class orator, magna cum laude*

William Hugh McCord

William Earl Martin

Muriel Florence Mitchell, *magna cum laude*

John William Painter

Lena Frances Pardue

Annie Lewis Pleasants

Erma Madison Russell, *cum laude*

Herbert Whitelaw Samsel

Franke Sheddan, *cum laude*

Augustus Sisk

Esther Apharine Striplin

Margaret Sutton Sugg

Marguerite Sutton, *magna cum laude*

Stacie Arbeely Tedford

Alice Elizabeth Wright

## GRADUATE IN BIBLE TRAINING
George Ella Simpson

## GRADUATES IN HOME ECONOMICS

Ethel Leona Burchfiel

Edna McBee Foster

Margaret Mason Jones

Nona Marie Wilson

## POST-GRADUATES IN PIANO

Jonnie Willie Catlett

Winifred Joy Decker

Lucy Genevieve Gibson

Sara Louise Kittrell

Bernice Lee Lowry

Lena Frances Pardue

Margaret Sutton Sugg

## GRADUATE IN PIANO
Celia Ellen Rough

## POST-GRADUATE IN VOICE
Mary Kate Rankin

## GRADUATES IN EXPRESSION

Muriel Florence Mitchell        Erma Madison Russell

## GRADUATE IN PUBLIC SPEAKING
Mark Blaine Crum

# REGISTER OF STUDENTS

## College Department

### SENIOR CLASS

ANDERSON, ROY RITTER.......... Loudon ........... Social Science
BASSETT, MARGARET............. Newport, Pa........ Modern Languages
BROCKLEHURST, ZEORA MONTEZ... Mercer, Pa......... General
BRYSON, ALTON DAVIS........... Whitwell .......... Mathematics
COOPER, FINIS GASTON.......... Gastonburg, Ala..... Mathematics
DAWSON, HORACE................ South Knoxville..... Classical
FERNTHEIL, HARRY HENRY....... Cincinnati, O........ Classical
FISHER, MATTIE MILDRED........ Lewisburg ......... Modern Languages
GIBSON, LUCY GENEVIEVE......... DeSoto, Mo......... General
HENRY, ELIZABETH AMY......... Elizabeth, N. J...... Classical
JORDAN, HERBERT JOSEPH........ Beverly, N. J....... Classical
KNAPP, JOSEPHINE.............. Maryville .......... Mathematics
LLOYD, GLEN ALFRED............ Fort Duchesne, Utah. General
LOGAN, ONESSUS HORNER........ Persia ............. General
MILES, MARY................... Knoxville, R. D. 10.. Modern Languages
MOSELEY, ELEANOR DORTCH....... Kissimmee, Fla...... General
RICHARDS, ANDREW.............. Leith, Scotland...... General
SCRUGGS, FRANK HEISKELL....... Sweetwater ........ General
SIMPSON, GEORGE ELLA.......... Rowland .......... General
TAYLOR, ROBERT LANDON........ New Market........ General
TURNER, JAMES HASKEW........ Maryville, R. D. 1'.. General
WATKINS, BENJAMIN EDWARD.... Indian Springs, Ga.. Science
WEBSTER, ALFRED HARRISON...... Kingston, R. D. 5... Social Science
WILLIAMS, DECK CHRISTOPHER... Cosby ............. General
WILSON, BERTHA MARY......... Maryville .......... General

### JUNIOR CLASS

ADAMS, ROBERT WRIGHT......... Burnsville, N. C..... General
ASBURY, EVELYN................ Crawfordville, Ga.... General
BAILEY, DAVIE GRACE........... Baileyton .......... Classical
BRIGGS, DAVID HEZEKIAH........ Marshall, N. C...... General
BROWN, HELEN ROSALIE......... Brooklyn, N. Y...... Classical
BURCHFIEL, ETHEL LEONA........ Dandridge .......... Science
CAGLE, FRED HOBART............ Englewood ......... Mathematics
CLAYTON, LUCRETIA DEXTER...... Industrial, W. Va.... General

Cox, Jasper Morgan.............Spencer, W. Va..... General
Davis, Edith Millard............Miller Place, N. Y... General
Edgemon, Charles Louis.......Englewood ........ General
Garrison, William Reid.......Derita, N. C......... General
Guess, Katherine Eloise........Chesterfield, S. C.... General
Hayes, William Young.........Woodstock, Ala...... General
Holmes, William Bryan, Jr....Birmingham, Ala.... General
House, Harvey Walter..........San Diego, Calif..... General
Howard, Adah Henley.........Maryville, R. D. 1... General
James, Ernest Kelly...........Maple Hill, N. C..... General
Kiger, John Herbert...........Wheeling, W. Va.... Eng. Lit. and History
LaRue, Claude Smith..........LaGrange, Ind....... General
Lewis, Mary Kate..............Meridian, Miss...... General
Logan, Rosa Emma.............Persia ............. Bible Training
McConnell, Thomas Lamar....Maryville, R. D. 6... Mathematics
McCurry, Luther Russell.......Mosheim .......... Science
Miles, Emma...................Knoxville, R. D. 10.. Modern Languages
Newell, Helen Elizabeth.......Chattanooga ........ Modern Languages
Pardue, Jamie Maude..........Sweetwater ......... Classical
Park, Carmen..................Culleoka ........... General
Paul, Ruby....................Maryville .......... General
Purdy, Jason G................Maryville .......... Classical
Ritchie, Eva ..................Biggsville, Ill........ General
Sheffey, Thomas Phillips......Maryville .......... Mathematics
Smith, Ralph Elisha...........Harlan, Ky......... Mathematics
Thompson, Lillian Marie.......Mercer, Pa.......... General
Thompson, Mary Estelle.......Salem, Ind.......... General
Townsend, Marietta Porter....South Plainfield, N. J. Classical
Wilkinson, Carrie Tipton......Maryville, R. D. 6... General
Wilkinson, Margaret Catharine Maryville, R. D. 6... General
Wilson, Wildus Gail...........Sidney, O.......... General

## SOPHOMORE CLASS

Baird, Daniel E................Elk Valley.......... General
Barbour, Myron Froome.......Aurora, Ind......... General
Bartlett, Miriam Jane.........Sault Ste.Marie,Mich. General
Bledsoe, Nelle ................Lynnville .......... Classical
Bogart, Claudia ..............Hampton, N. J...... General
Bogart, Mary Elmira..........Hampton, N. J...... Science
Brown, Horace Earl...........Maryville .......... Classical
Callahan, George Brandle.....Erwin ............. General
Carpenter, Della .............Peoples, Ky........ General
Chang, Tien Ze...............Hangchow, China.... General
Corry, Annie Irrovia..........Siloam, Ga......... General

CRESWELL, JESSIE ANNE......... Bluefield, W. Va..... Mathematics
CRESWELL, MARY DAVIS.......... Maryville .......... General
DILLINGHAM, LEONORA BELLE..... Barnardsville, N. C.. General
DOLVIN, AGNES IRENE............ Siloam, Ga.......... Eng. Lit. and History
DRAKE, THEODORE CURRY........ Maryville .......... Social Science
FLOYD, LONA MILDRED............ Greenville, Ill........ Modern Languages
FRATER, NOTIE FANCHER......... Sparta ............. General
GAMBLE, HELEN REBECCA......... Maryville, R. D. 6... General
GEORGES, JOEL SAMUEL.......... Ourmiah, Persia..... Mathematics
GIBBONS, ELDRED HARRIS........ Maryville .......... General
GIBSON, WILLIAM D....:....... Elk Valley.......... General
HAMILTON, MATTIE ............. McKenzie .......... General
HAMILTON, VINCENT BAKER...... Church Hill........ Science
HARTMAN, MARY JANE........... Rockport, Ind....... Modern Languages
HAYES, HATTIE IRENE........... Woodstock, Ala..... General
HAYES, MARY LOUISE........... Woodstock, Ala..... General
HENRY, BESSIE LEE.............. Maryville, R. D. 2... General
HENRY, FRANCES MARION....... Elizabeth, N. J...... Social Science
HOWELL, STACEY FRANCIS....... Snow Shoe, Pa...... Science
HUFF, EDMOND JEREMIAH........ Harlan, Ky.......... General
HUNTER, MINNIE ANNE......:.. Pine Knob, W. Va... General
JACKSON, ELIZABETH LUCRETIA... Concord ............ Modern Languages
JOHNSON, JOHN GUTHRIE:........ Jemison, Ala........ General
JOHNSON, LICIA ................ Graysville .......... General
KRESPACH, MARIAN DOROTHY..... Princeton, N. J...... Modern Languages
LEWIS, HELEN ................. Meridian, Miss...... Classical
LIPPERT, WILLIAM KEMPER....... Williamsburg, O..... Classical
MCCAMPBELL, VERA CLEO........ Knoxville, R. D. 6... General
MCCLANAHAN, ALBION AMZI, JR. Springfield ......... General
MCGRANAHAN, ISABEL .......... Knoxville .......... General
MCIVER, WILLODINE ............ Cordele, Ga........ General
MCLAUGHLIN, FRANK SHERMAN... Mifflin, Pa.......... Classical
MARION, LESTER LAFAYETTE...... Blountville ......... Science
MARTIN, JAMES ................ Mansfield, O........ Classical
MOORE, EDITH WILSON.......... Maryville .......... Classical
MORTON, JANE PENMAN.......... National, Md....... General
MOSELEY, MARY CELESTE........ Kissimmee, Fla...... Eng. Lit. and History
MOULTON, DENZIL WILLIAM...... Fall Branch........ Mathematics
NEWTON, WINSTON CORDELIA..... Harriman .......... Modern Languages
PARK, GEORGE HILLARY.......... Culleoka ........... Science
PLEASANTS, MAMIE ENNIS....... Roxboro, N. C....... Modern Languages
POLK, CERENA SUE.............. Maryville, R. D. 5... General
PRICE, ALBERT MARVIN.......... Huntington, W. Va.. Science
PURDY, MADRITH JEANNETTE...... Maryville .......... General
RICE, MABEL DOROTHY.......... Osborn, O.......... General

RIDGWAY, FRANCES CATHERINE ... Palatka, Fla......... General
SHEDDAN, CARRIE BELLE......... DeLand, Fla......... General
STANTON, OSCAR ............... Marshall, N. C..... Social Science
STUMP, UGEE .................. Flatwoods, W. Va... Modern Languages
SUSONG, SUELLA ............... Walland ............ General
TEDFORD, HELEN BOND............ Concord :.......... General
TURNER, COLA CHRISTINE........ Auburn, Ky......... Science
TURNER, HELENA RIVERS......... Auburn, Ky......... Science
WALKER, HENRY MOODY.......... Athens, Ala......... General
WEBB, OCEY BLANCHE........... Townsend .......... Modern Languages
WELLS, EVA BRYAN............. Springfield ......... General
WILSON, BEATRICE RUTH......... Ashland, Ala........ General

## FRESHMAN CLASS

ARMENTROUT, MARY EMMA....... White Pine.......... Science
BAILEY, BLANCHE RUSH......... Baileyton .......... General
BARTLETT, ROBERT MERRILL....... Sault Ste.Marie,Mich. General
BEARD, DELEMO LEETASSEE........ Staunton, Va........ General
BECK, DEWEY MARIAN........... Erwin ............. General
BELT, ROBERT LEROY............. Wellsville .......... General
BILLS, HAROLD LONG............. Lewisburg .......... General
BOWERS, CARL ADELBERT......... Elizabethton ....... General
BROWN, JESSIE HASTIE........... Cleveland .......... General
BROWN, THERON NELSON........ Maryville, R. D. 5... General
BUCHANAN, PERCY WILSON...... Kobe, Japan........ Classical
BURKHART, WILLIAM SHERMAN.. Smith, Ky.......... General
CAMPBELL, LILLIE BELLE......... Elizabethton ....... General
CARD, ERA MARGUERITE.......... Chattanooga ....... General
CARLOCK, ANNE ELIZA.......... Livingston ......... General
CLAYTON, ASHTON BAYARD....... Industrial, W. Va.... General
CLAYTON, RUTH ................ Romulus, N. Y...... Eng. Lit. and History
CLEMENS, ROBERT BROADY........ Maryville .......... General
CLEVELAND, HAZEL FRANCES...... Cambridge, N. Y.... Bible Training
COPELAND, MAYBLE ELIZABETH ... Monterey .......... General
CORTNER, AUBREY STANLEY....... Cortner ............ General
COTTON, JARVIS MADISON......... Erwin ............. General
CURTIS, TINIE ................. Shelbyville ......... General
CUTLER, MABLE ................ Greenfield .......... Home Economics
DAMIANO, CARL EUGENE........ Fairmont, W. Va.... General
DAWSON, ELSIE ELMORE.......... South Knoxville..... General
DECKER, WINIFRED JOY........... Kiln, Miss.......... Eng. Lit. and History
FARMER, MOSS .................. McKee, Ky.......... Mathematics
FISHER, MARGARET ............. Lewisburg .......... General
FOSTER, SAMUEL RAY........... Maryville .......... General

GILBERT, IDA ESTELLA............Chattanooga ........General
GILLESPIE, EDWARD ELDEN........Weston, O..........General
GILLESPIE, GEORGE BENTON.......Walland ............General
GRAY, JESSE ALLEN..............Wytheville, Va.....Mathematics
GRAY, LEVEN DARBY..............Ferris, Tex.........Mathematics
GRIBBLE, EMMA LOUISE..........Acworth, Ga.........General
HADDOX, TROY MAE..............Knoxville, R. D. 3...Eng. Lit. and History
HALL, VIVIAN MARZEE...........Lynnville ..........General
HARRIS, LENA .................Isabella ............Modern Languages
HIBBERT, JEANNETTE ............Maryville ..........Classical
HICKEY, FRANCES WILLARD.......Jonesboro ..........General
HITE, JOHN SYDNEY..............Fairfield, Va.......General
HITE, MAUDE CLEMENCE.........Fairfield, Va.......General
HOWELL, GEORGE DEWEY..........Branchville, N. J....Classical
HUDSON, MARTHA ELISABETH.....Montreat, N. C......Bible Training
HUSKEY, ISAAC LEMEN...........Sevierville, R. D. 9..General
JACKSON, ETHEL ISABEL..........Harriman ..........General
JUSTICE, SUSAN DUDLEY.........Pittsburgh, Pa.......General
KENNEDY, JOHN PERRY..........Birmingham, Ala....General
KIRKPATRICK, KARL ............Persia .............General
LIPPERT, NELLY ELIZABETH.......Cincinnati, O.......General
LIVINGSTON, ANNA LENA.........Monterey ..........General
LIVINGSTON, MAGGIE MAE........Monterey ..........General
LLOYD, HAL LAFAYETTE..........Fort Duchesne, Utah. General
LUDMAN, GRACE JOSSELYN.......Fulton, O..........General
MCCLARY, SAMUEL WASHINGTON. Ocoee .............General
MCCONKEY, VIRGINIA ELIZABETH. Maryville ..........General
MCKINNEY, ESTHER ADELLA......Wheat .............Education
MASON, MARY JANE YOUNG......Woodstock, Ala.....General
MINTER, MAMIE SUE............Monticello, Ga......General
MONTGOMERY, EMILY ...........Piqua, O...........General
MONTGOMERY, ESTHER ..........Piqua, O...........General
MONTGOMERY, ORMA ............Fayetteville .........General
NELSON, CAROLYN FANSON.......Assumption, Ill......General
NUCKOLS, THERESA SUE.........Cleburne, Tex.......General
OLIVER, LUCILE BARBARA........Maryville ..........General
PEERY, JAMES HARVEY..........Maryville, R. D. 8...General
PETERS, JACOB BURTON..........Friendsville ........General
PODESTA, NICHOLAS ARTHUR......Festus, Mo.........Pre-Medical
PRENTIS, LILLIAN MARY.........Kissimmee, Fla......General
PURDY, ELMA ALETHA...........Maryville ..........General
PUTMAN, LAURA EMILY.........Barker, N. Y.......Social Science
ROBISON, MARTHA ELIZABETH.....Birmingham, Ala....Education
RUSSELL, BARBARA EILEEN.......Burlington .........Home Economics
SHARP, ANNIE MAE.............Bearden ...........Home Economics

SHERROD, CLIFFORD CARTER........Louisville ...........General
SIMMONS, CHARLES WESLEY......Johnsonville ........General
SIZER, EDWIN MARZEL...........Philadelphia ........Science
SMITH, ADA FRANCES...........Morristown .........General
SMITH, DANIEL BOONE...........Smith, Ky...........General
STACY, MATTIE LOU.............Sparta .............General
STRIPLIN, MILDRED .............Gurley, Ala.........General
SULLINGER, MARGUERITE .........Maryville ...........General
TETEDOUX, GENEVIEVE APOLLINE..Norwood, O.........General
WARE, LELA AGNES..............Birmingham, Ala....Science
WARREN, CECIL RHEA...........Fall Branch.........General
WATT, FLOYD RODGERS...........Loudon ............Classical
WEBB, DIXIE LEE...............Knoxville, R. D. 2...General
WEISBECKER, HOMER GEORGE......Fort Wayne, Ind....General
WHITEHEAD, STANLEY HERMAN..Erwin .............General
WHITTLE, MARY ALMA..........Knoxville, R. D. 12..General
WILLIAMS, EUGENE MONROE......Maryville ...........Mathematics
WILLIAMS, JOHN OLLIE..........Columbia ...........General
WILLIAMS, LAILA IRENE.........Crawfordsville, Ind..General
WILSON, LAMAR SILSBY..........Maryville ...........General
WITHERSPOON, MANIE WALKER...Kissimmee, Fla.....General
YOUNG, ROY FELTON............Atlanta, Ga.........General

## IRREGULAR COLLEGIATE STUDENTS

BULLOCK, EUNICE LURA..........Sabanno, Tex........Education
BUTLER, LOIS MARIE.............Crawfordsville, Ind..General
CAMPBELL, ALFRED RUSSELL......Greenville, Tex......General
CAUGHRON, SYDNEY CANNON.....New Market........General
CAUGHRON, WILLIAM ALVIS......New Market........General
COVERT, ESTHER GRACE..........Jeffersonville, Ind...General
CROSS, SHELBY CECIL............Columbiana, Ala.....General
CRUM, MIRIAM .................Charlestown, Ind....General
DAVIDSON, LESLIE EUGENE........Kingston ...........General
DEARING, ELIZABETH BUST.......Potosi, Mo..........General
DEYTON, JASON BASIL............Forbes, N. C........General
DILWORTH, CHARLES WINFORD....Rienzi, Miss.........General
DORSEY, ANNIE ELIZABETH.......Gainesville, Fla......General
DOUGHTY, SAM RODGERS..........Concord ...........General
EAGLETON, DAVID PARKS..........Maryville ...........General
FINE, ADDIE LOIS................Dandridge ..........Mathematics
GIBBONS, EVELYN MIGNON.......Maryville ...........General
GREEN, DESTHER ANN...........Sabanno, Tex.......General
GRIFFIN, OLGA AILEEN...........McKinney, Tex......General
HARMS, JEAN .................Albertville, Ala......General

HARRIS, GEORGE ALLMAN.........Lewisburg ..........General
HARTUNG, MABEL DAVIDSON......Albany, Ala.........General
HENDERSON, OWEN ..............Cohutta, Ga.........General
HIGGINBOTHAM, ADA VALLE.......Fertile, Mo.........General
HITE, ROBERT EDWARD, JR........Fairfield, Va........General
HORTON, HELEN ELIZABETH......Harriman ...........General
HUFFSTETLER, IRL ..............Maryville ..........General
JOHNSON, MEADE MILTON........Etowah ............General
LANGE, STANLEY CHARLES........Cincinnati, O........Classical
LLOYD, MARJORIE GRACE.........Fredonia, Ky........General
LOFT, ERNEST EDMUND..........London, England....General
McCURRY, ADDIE MAE...........Mosheim ...........General
MARCHANT, EDITH LORENE......Ducktown ..........General
MARCHANT, MAUD LUCILLE......Ducktown ..........General
MILLER, CEDRIC VERDI...........Philadelphia, Pa.....Classical
PUGH, GEORGE LEONIDAS.........Asheville, N. C.....General
REECE, RALEIGH VALENTINE......Butler .............General
RICKS, MELVIN BYRON...........Kannapolis, N. C....General
ROBERTS, ROLAND DOUGLAS......Ferris, Tex.........General
ROGERS, LOMA LAVYTA..........Jellico .............Home Economics
RYDER, MARY ALVA.............Wytheville, Va......General
SMITH, HAROLD EDWARD........Maywood, Ill.......Science
SPECK, FRANCES ELORA..........Monterey ..........Home Economics
TEMPLIN, AUGUSTA MARIE......Morristown ........General
WAGNER, HARRY WILLIAM..:....Portsmouth, O......General
WICKS, JOSEPHINE ELIZABETH....Chattanooga ........Bible Training
WILSON, DORIS MAE.............Ashland, Ala........General
WITHERSPOON, JOHN KNOX......Kissimmee, Fla......Science
WOLFE, MARY WINIFRED........Piney Flats.........Home Economics
ZIRKLE, GEORGE CAMPBELL.......Dandridge ..........Mathematics
ZUMSTEIN, IDA ANNA...........Wartburg ..........Home Economics

## COLLEGE SPECIAL STUDENTS

ADAMS, ELMER NEWTON.........Maryville ...........Mathematics
BROTHERS, EDITH MAE...........Columbus, O........Music
CHASE, ALLENE MILDRED........Peekskill, N. Y.....Bible Training
DOCTOR, ETHEL RUSSELL.........Lonsdale, R. I.......Bible Training
GEORGE, EDWINA ...............Maryville ..........Music
GIBSON, CHAPMAN J.............Maryville ..........Officers Training
HAWORTH, TAYLOR EARL.........New Market.......General
HENRY, ANN ...................Maryville, R. D. 2...Art
LaRUE, ANNIE LAURIE...........Parrottsville ........General
McCONNELL, MAE LUCILLE.......Kingsport ..........Home Economics
MAXEY, JAMES TOOLE...........Maryville ..........Officers Training

MOORE, EMMA ................... North Maryville..... General
MOORE, JOHN WYNDHAM......... McClellanville, S. C... General
PAUL, GEORGE HURST........... Maryville ...........: General
PRYOR, ASA ALBERT.............. Mason, Mich........ General
SINGLETON, MARTHA JACKSON.... Maryville ........... Expression
TWEED, JANCER LAWRENCE, B.A.. Maryville ........... Officers Training
WILLIAMSON, RUTH ELIZABETH... Maryville ........... Music

## Preparatory Department

### FOURTH YEAR CLASS

ADAMS, J. EDGAR................ Mountain City....... Classical
BLACK, NORMAN McKINLEY...... Harrisburg, N. C.... Classical
BONIFACIUS, CARL WALTER....... Wartburg .......... Classical
CALDWELL, EDITH FAWN......... Maryville ........... General
CRAIG, RINEY .................. Sharps Chapel....... Classical
ELLIS, ELIZABETH .............. Maryville .......... Classical
ELLIS, HORACE KNOX........... Maryville .......... Classical
FORD, RUFUS LAFAYETTE......... Hartford .......... Classical
GREENLEE, RUTH McENTIRE...... Old Fort, N. C...... Classical
HARMAN, LOUIS ELMORE......... Russellville, O....... Classical
HEMPHILL, IDELLA .............. Morris, Ala........ Classical
HENDERSON, PAUL .............. Cohutta, Ga........ Classical
HICKMAN, RUSH STROUP........ Ensley, Ala......... Classical
HUMPHRIES, CORIN EZRA........ Toyah, Tex......... Classical
JONES, ELIZABETH JANE......... Maryville .......... Classical
LATIMER, CHARLES YEATMAN..... Lancing ........... Classical
LEGG, JOHN WALLACE........... Jefferson City....... General
LEQUIRE, JENNIE BELLE......... Walland ............ Classical
LEWIS, FRED CORNETT........... Harlan, Ky......... Classical
LUDMAN, WILLIAM BROWN...... Fulton, O.......... Classical
McCALL, RUTH ................. Knoxville, R. D. 10.. Classical
McCALL, STELLA LOVE...........: Maryville .......... Classical
McDONALD, CLARA BEATRICE..... Sallisaw, Okla....... Classical
McGRATH, HOWARD DIXON....... New York, N. Y.... Classical
McNUTT, MARY LAWSON........ Maryville .......... Classical
McNUTT, MOSES MADISON........ Concord ........... Classical
MARSHALL, BEATRICE IONE....... Greenwich, Conn.... Classical
MEASAMER, MURRY BRYANT...... Concord, N. C....... Classical
MILLS, MARY IVA.............. Greenback .......... Classical
MOMARY, WILLIAM ROSTOM...... Homs, Syria........ Classical
PEARSON, HARRY MARVIN ....... Minnieville, Va...... Classical
PHILLIPS, RAYMOND FONTAINE ... McKenzie .......... Classical
RATCLIFF, CLELAND KINLOCK..... King George, Va.... Classical

RUSSELL, NANCY AILEEN......... Rockford ............ Classical
RUSSELL, NELLE MARGARET....... Rockford ............ Classical
SCHNEIDER, AILEEN DIXIE........ Mount Vernon, Ind.. General
SEATON, REBECCA ALENE......... Maryville ............ Classical
STEARNS, WILLIAM EDGAR......... Weston, O.......... Classical
STINNETT, SARAH ANN .......... Townsend .......... Classical
STRIPLIN, ORAMANTOR ELIZABETH. Gurley, Ala.......... Classical
TEDFORD, HUGH CRAIG........... Maryville ........... General
WALLER, JANE KNOX............. Maryville ........... Classical
WARWICK, EMALENE EDITH ...... Corryton ............ Classical
WATTENBARGER, CLARA ELLEN.... Erwin ............. Classical
WELLS, JAMES LAWRENCE........ Maryville ........... General
WEST, CLYDE ECKLES............ Maryville, R. D. 4... General
WILLIAMS, RACHEL MAYME....... Maryville, R. D. 4... Classical
WITZEL, EMA .................. Blue Ridge, Ga...... Classical

## THIRD YEAR CLASS

ANDERSON, MARY RHEA.......... Maryville ........... Classical
ANDERSON, WILLIAM HARRIS..... Maryville ........... Classical
ANDES, ALICE MEANS............ Sanford, Fla....... Classical
ARNOTT, STELLA VIRGO.......... Persia .............. Classical
BASSEL, MARY ELIZABETH........ Maryville ........... Classical
BEVAN, JAMES J................ Westbourne ........ Classical
BIGELOW, MARY ELIZABETH....... Birmingham, Ala.... Classical
BLACK, MARY FRANCES........... Patterson, Mo....... Classical
BOWERS, EDWARD LOCKETT....... Maryville, R. D. 4... Classical
BREWER, MILDRED EDNA.......... Walland ............ General
BROWN, STACIE PAULINE......... Moraine ............ General
BUCKNER, CLAUDE SMITH........ Maynardville ....... Classical
BURCHFIELD, DANIEL LUTHER..... Maryville ........... Classical
CALDWELL, EDWARD ALEXANDER... Maryville ........... Classical
CATES, CHARLOTTE WILKINSON ... Maryville, R. D. 3....Classical
CHANDLER, MARGARET McELWEE... Maryville ........... Classical
CLEMENS, ADELINE TURRELL...... Maryville ........... Classical
COLEMAN, EBERT ELLSWORTH..... Maryville ........... Classical
COLLINS, FLORENCE NICOL........ Montgomery, Ala.... Classical
COLLINS, MARGARET CHRISTINE ... Montgomery, Ala.... Classical
COPELAND, FRANCES IMOGENE..... Monterey ........... Classical
CORLEY, GEORGE WILLIAM........ Alexandria ......... Classical
COULTER, THEODORE MONROE...... Walland ............ Classical
CROSS, SAM YOUNG.............. Oliver Springs....... Classical
DOLVIN, MARY KEY.............. Siloam, Ga.......... Classical
EDENS, JOHN J................. Bokchito, Okla...... General
ELLIS, CHARLES FRANCIS......... Maryville, R. D. 6... Classical

FINCH, LEITA BELLE............Moore, S. C.........Classical
FOWLER, HAMMOND ............Rockwood ..........Classical
GARNER, JOHN ................Maryville ..........Classical
GARREN, BERTHA ...............Vonore ...........Classical
GIBSON, ROSCOE KENNEDY.......Boyds Creek........Classical
GORHAM, REUEL HADEN.........Franklin, Ky........Classical
GRANT, LLOYD EARL.............Dorothy, W. Va.....Classical
GREENLEE, JOSEPH LOGAN........Old Fort, N. C......Classical
GRIFFITH, GERTRUDE MITCHELL...Oliver Springs.......Classical
GRIFFITH, MINNIE BELLE.........Moraine ...........General
HALE, GEORGE LAFAYETTE........Russellville .........Classical
HARRISON, WALLACE ............Maryville ..........Classical
HEARD, MARY ETHEL............Detroit, Mich........Classical
HERNDON, LEE ROY.............Turin, Ky...........Classical
HITCH, MILDRED ..............Louisville, R. D. 2...Classical
HUFFAKER, IRA REGINALD.......Knoxville, R. D. 14..Classical
HURST, RELLA VICTOR...........Sevierville, R. D. 8..Classical
JAMISON, BERTHA JEANNETTA....Piqua, O............General
JONES, BESS DALE..............Farrell, Miss........General
JONES, EDWIN LESLIE...........Charlestown, Ind....Classical
JONES, EMORY MITCHELL.........Indian Springs......Classical
KING, EARL C.................Louisville ..........Classical
KING, RAYMOND MCKINLEY......Louisville ..........Classical
KINGINS, PAUL JUDSON..........Bumpus Mills.......Classical
LAWSON, ORA REBECCA..........Sevierville ..........General
LEYSHON, HAROLD IRWIN........Knoxville ..........Classical
McCALL, HELEN CAROLYN........Maryville, R. D. 8...Classical
McCURRY, WILLIAM ERNEST......Mosheim ..........Classical
McNUTT, GRACE AZALIA........Maryville ..........Classical
McNUTT, ROBERT LYLE..........Maryville ..........Classical
MARION, HENRY FRANK.........Blountville .........Classical
MINARIK, FRANK STUYVESANT...New York, N. Y....Classical
MONTGOMERY, HETTIE SUE.......Maryville ..........Classical
MOORE, CHESTER ARTHUR........Mildred, Ky.........Classical
MOORE, FRANCES GRACE.........Moore, S. C.........Classical
MOORE, SARAH AUGUSTA........Moore, S. C.........Classical
MULLENDORE, FRANK HALE.......Sevierville .........Classical
MUSICK, ABRAHAM LINCOLN.....Sutton, Ky.........Classical
NEWTON, RUTH ELIZABETH.......Harriman ..........Classical
NICELY, LULA VIRGINIA.........Washburn ..........General
PARKS, JOHN LINDSEY..........Barium Springs, N. C. Classical
PHILLIPS, CLYDE ROBERT........Blountville .........Classical
POAGUE, LEAH MAUDE..........Graysville ..........Classical
RENDON, REBECCA AMELIA.......Las Vegas, N. M....Classical
RHEA, MARY ELSIE.............Harlan, Ky.........Classical

ROBINSON, FOUNT ............... Liberty ............. Classical
SAMSEL, ANNE LAURIE.......... Tate .............. Classical
SETTLE, GUY DENNIS............. Maryville .......... Classical
SIMPSON, CORA LEILA............ Knoxville .......... General
SPECK, CALLYE AMELIA.......... Monterey .......... Classical
THOMPSON, RUBY LILLIAN....... Maryville, R. D. 5... Classical
TROTTER, JONNIE ALICE.......... Maryville .......... Classical
TURNER, HORACE IRVING......... Philadelphia, Miss... General
WALKER, JOE KNAFFLE........... Maryville .......... General
WATERS, MAE .................. Maryville .......... General
WELLS, ARTHUR EUGENE......... Maryville .......... Classical
WILEY, VELMA SMITH........... Lexington, Ky....... Classical
WILLIAMS, MATILDA BELLE....... Maryville, R. D. 4... Classical
WRIGHT, EMILY OLIVER.......... Augusta, Ga........ Classical

## SECOND YEAR CLASS

ANDERSON, IVA BELLE............ Knoxville, R. D. 11.. Classical
ARMSTRONG, ANNIE ARTHUR..... Surgoinsville ....... Classical
AULT, VERA MAE................ Knoxville, R. D. 6... General
BASSEL, JOHN BURR............. Maryville .......... Classical
BEST, CHARLES BRADFORD........ Mint .............. General
BICKNELL, ROBERT COOKE........ Maryville .......... General
BLACK, JOHN DAWSON........... Greenback .......... Classical
BLACK, SADIE ESTELLE........... Harrisburg, N. C.... Classical
BLANK, GRACE JOSEPHINE........ Chicago, Ill......... Classical
BOGGS, KARL K................. Typo, Ky............ General
BURKHART, HENRY CLAY......... Smith, Ky........... Classical
CALDERWOOD, REBECCA .......... Alcoa ............. Classical
CALDWELL, RUTH ODESSA........ Louisville, R. D. 2... Classical
CHANDLER, JOHN RICHARD........ Maryville .......... Classical
CLEVENGER, SHELL ............. Newport .......... General
CLEVENGER, WALTER THOMAS..... Newport .......... General
COLEMAN, GEORGE ELDREDGE...... East Moline, Ill...... Classical
COPELAND, SUSIE KATHERINE..... Monterey .......... Classical
COPENHAVER, MILDRED REBECCA... Rock Island........ Classical
CORLEY, EDWIN BOYD............ Alexandria ........ General
CORRY, FLOYD THOMAS.......... Siloam, Ga......... General
COVINGTON, WILLIAM HENRY..... Meridian, Miss...... General
DELLINGER, WILLIAM HARRY..... Kannapolis, N. C.... Classical
DENNY, GEORGE HAROLD......... Buffalo Valley....... Classical
DRAKE, MARGARET ELIZABETH.... Maryville .......... Classical
DUNLAP, LILLIAN LUCILE........ Maryville .......... Classical
ERWIN, JULIAN G............... Old Fort........... Classical
FAUBION, MARY WOOD........... Maryville, R. D. 8....General
FOWLER, MINA BLANCHE......... Philadelphia ........ Classical

FOWLER, ROY NEIL.............. Maryville .......... Classical
FOWLER, SARA JOSEPHINE........ Philadelphia ........ Classical
FRENCH, EDNA ALMA............ Maryville, R. D. 4... Classical
FROW, ROBERT PORTER........... Maryville .......... General
FURMAN, DELBERT ............. Oakdale ........... Classical
GABANY, VICTOR CARL........... Dorothy, W. Va..... Classical
GAMBLE, RUTH ................ Maryville, R. D. 6... Classical
GIBBONS, AVERELL SCHELL....... Maryville .......... Classical
GILLESPIE, ANNABELLE .......... Walland ........... Classical
GILLESPIE, JESSE CARSON........ Maryville .......... Classical
GLEASON, CHAUNCEY ROLLAND... Glen Mary......... Classical
HAMBY, GEORGE ............... Hiwassee, N. C..... Classical
HANEY, ALON CARL............. Old Fort, N. C..... Classical
HARRISON, NEVA .............. Maryville, R. D. 8... Classical
HENRY, JONNIE BELLE........... Maryville .......... Classical
HAUK, JONNIE WANDA........... Fountain City....... General
HUGGINS, ANDREW FRANCIS...... Dandridge ......... General·
HUNTER, JOHN CLIFFORD........ Day Book, N. C..... Classical
HUNTER, ROBERT SHERRILL....... Burnsville, N. C..... Classical
JELLICORSE, CHARLES EDWARD, JR...Davidson ........... General
KESTERSON, JOHN WASHINGTON.. Maryville .......... General
KITTRELL, BEULAH MAE.......... Maryville .......... Classical
LEGG, OLIVER MILLER............ Jefferson City....... Classical
LEWIS, ELLA MARY............. Harlan, Ky......... Classical
LITTERER, MARY EVANS.......... Maryville .......... Classical
LOWE, ISABELLE ................ Vose .............. Classical
LOWRY, FRANK HOUSTON........ Madisonville ........ General
MCCALL, ROY ALEXANDER........ Maryville .......... Classical
MCCARTER, LULA MAE........... Gatlinburg .......... Classical
MCCOLLUM, DOROTHY REBA...... Vonore ............ Classical
MCCOLLUM, RUBY LENA......... Vonore ............ Classical
MCCONKEY, JOHN ROSS.......... Maryville .......... Classical
MCCULLEY, MARY FLORENCE..... Maryville .......... General
MCGINLEY, ELIZABETH JEANETTE...Maryville .......... Classical
MCGINLEY, NANNIE BARUM...... Maryville .......... General
MCGINLEY, SUSIE LUELLA....... Maryville .......... Classical
MCMAHAN, IVA MARTHA........ Maryville .......... Classical
MCMURRAY, JONNIE FOUTE....... Chilhowee .......... Classical
MAY, MONTGOMERY, JR.......... Maryville .......... Classical
MITCHELL, SARAH ELIZABETH .... Greensburg, Ky...... Classical
MONTGOMERY, JOHN EDWARD..... Knoxville, R. D. 10.. Classical
MOORE, HORACE STRONG......... Maryville ·.......... Classical
NICKELL, ELLA MARIE........... Greenup, Ky........ General
NOE, AMELIA ROSE............. Harlan, Ky......... General
NUCHOLS, JOHN ELIJAH......... Maryville, R. D. 5... Classical

OGAN, RALPH WILSON.......... Cumberland, O...... Classical
PAINTER, DOROTHY CHRISTINE.... Maryville, R. D. 6... Classical
PAYNE, JENNINGS BRYAN........ Cross Rock, N. C.... General
PERRY, LYDIA HARDWICK......... Atlanta, Ga......... Classical
PORTER, CHARLES ABRAM......... Pittsburgh, Pa....... General
PRYOR, LIDA MAE.............. Maryville, R. D. 8... General
PUGH, LOUISE KEMON .......... Hyattsville, Md...... Classical
ROBBINS, EDGAR GUY............. Erwin ............. Classical
ROWAN, JAMES VICTOR.......... Maryville .......... Classical
ROWLETT, FAY OMER............. Medina ............ General
RUSSELL, BERTHA MAE.......... Rutledge ........... Classical
SAMSEL, MAUDE OPIE........... Tate .............. Classical
SCHAEFFER, LAVINIA MIRIAM..... Maryville .......... Classical
SCHOLL, ROY WALTER........... Ensley, Ala......... General
SEATON, ALFRED LEO............ Maryville .......... Classical
STAFFORD, DAVID BELL, JR....... Louisville, Ky...... Classical
STINER, EDGAR ELI.............. Sharps Chapel....... General
TAYLOR, EUNICE CLIFTON........ Greenup, Ky........ Classical
TIPTON, ANNIE ................ Townsend .......... General
TOOLE, CASSIE LUCILLE.......... Knoxville, R. D. 3... Classical
TRAMELL, LUTHER HOWARD....... Jellico ............ Classical
WALKER, NANNETTE ............ Athens, Ala......... Classical
WATERS, JAMES MARTIN......... Walland ........... Classical
WEBB, HUGH CHALMER......... Sevierville, R. D. 7.. Classical
WELLS, MINNIE MAE............ Maryville, R. D. 5... General
WHALEY, CARL ................ Oakdale ........... Classical
WRIGHT, NANCY LAWSON........ Augusta, Ga......... Classical

### FIRST YEAR CLASS

ADAMS, EBIE ................... Mint .............. General
AGNEW, NED HERMAN........... Newbern .......... General
ALEXANDER, RUBY TENNESSEE.... Greenback .......... Classical
ANDERSON, CAMPBELL HARRIS.... Greenback .......... Classical
ARCAY, ROBERTO ............... Havana, Cuba....... General
ARCHER, KELSO CLEOPHIS........ Maryville .......... General
AYRES, WINSTON MCKINLEY..... Jellico, R. D. 2...... Classical
BAILEY, BERTHA JUNE........... Harlan, Ky......... General
BALL, LEONARD CAM............. Harlan, Ky......... Classical
BARTLETT, CHARLES HARRAL...... Durant, Okla........ Classical
BENNETT, JOSEPH OSCAR......... Louisville, Miss...... General
BERNARD, ELIZA ANNA........... Baileyton .......... General
BERRY, ROBERT WILLSON......... Loudon ............ Classical
BEST, LENA RODELLA............. Mint .............. General
BLAIR, ANABEL WILLIAMS........ Maryville .......... Classical

BLANCO, MANUEL .............. Havana, Cuba....... General
BOHANAN, VELMA .............. Seymour .......... General
BOOZE, KARL CLIFFORD........... White Star, Ky...... General
BORING, ETHEL VINA............ Rasar ............. General
BORING, JAMES McCLELLEN....... Maryville ..........:General
BROWN, JAMES MORRISON, JR..... Maryville, R. D. 5... Classical
BROWN, MARY ALEXANDER....... Maryville, R. D. 5... Classical
BRYSON, EMORY SAMUEL........ Unaka, N. C......... Classical
BUQUO, MARY LOWRY........... Hot Springs, N. C... Classical
BUQUO, MORRIS GRAY............ Hot Springs, N. C... Classical
CALDWELL, HARRY .............. Maryville .......... General
CAMERON, FLORA ETHEL......... Washburn .......... General
CAMERON, JOSEPH LUTHER....... Townsend .......... Classical
CAMPELLO, JOSE .............. Havana, Cuba....... General
CAPPS, HIRAM CLYDE........... Bakerville .......... Classical
CAPPS, STELLA ................. Bakerville .......... Classical
CARPENTER, LOIS .............. Greenback .......... Classical
CASTRO, MANUEL .............. Havana, Cuba....... General
CLARK, WILLIAM REECE.......... Binfield ............. Classical
CLAYTON, SARAH ................ Romulus, N. Y...... Classical
CLEMENS, CHARLES ROYSTER...... Maryville .......... Classical
CLOYD, COEN CARUTH, JR........ Red Boiling Springs. Classical
COLLINS, NELL ELIZABETH........ Maryville , .......... Classical
COULTER, HUGH ALEXANDER...... Maryville .......... Classical
COULTER, LUCY GEORGE.......... Walland ............ Classical
DAVIS, MARY IDA............... Maryville .......... Classical
DAVIS, WILLIE MYRTLE........... Walland ............ General
DUFF, JOHN BUFORD............. Maryville .......... Classical
DUNLAP, WILLIAM OLIVER........ Maryville .......... Classical
ELLIS, EDITH LOUISE............ Maryville .......... General
EMERT, HETTIE ANDES.......... Sevierville .......... General
EMERT, IDA MAE................ Sevierville .......... General
ENLOE, RALPH WALKER.......... Sevierville .......... Classical
EWING, EMILY CAROLYN.......... Mattoon, Ill......... Classical
FERRER, MELCHOR .............. Havana, Cuba....... General
FORESTER, NANCY HELEN........ Harlan, Ky......... General
FOSTER, BRUCE ................. Dorothy, W. Va..... Classical
FOSTER, LEILA MAE............. Dorothy, W. Va..... Classical
FRANKLIN, SAM HORACE, JR...... Maryville .......... Classical
GAMBLE, JOSEPH MYERS.......... Seymour .......... Classical
GAMBLE, MARTHA .............. Seymour .......... Classical
GLENN, CAMILLE HUGHES........ Knoxville .......... General
GODDARD, JAMES LOUIS.......... Maryville, R. D. 1... Classical
GODDARD, RAYMOND ............ Knoxville, R. D. 13.. Classical
GRAHAM, MARGARET ELLEN....... New Market........ Classical

GRIFFIN, CARRIE ALLERA............ Washington, Ga........ Classical
HAMPTON, GLADYS DORIS......... Skull Mill, N. C..... Classical
HANCOX, WILLIAM ARTHUR...... Walland ............ Classical
HARRISON, BERNICE BEATRICE..... Maryville ........... General
HARRISON, FRANK ERASTUS...... Maryville ........... General
HARRISON, GEORGIA EVA......... Maryville ........... General
HEADRICK, BELLE ................. Seymour ........... General
HENRY, MARY ELIZABETH........ Maryville ........... Classical
HILL, HOWARD TERELIUS......... Maryville ........... General
HITCH, FRANKIE ................. Maryville, R. D. 4... General
HITCH, MARY ELLEN............. Maryville, R. D. 5... General
HOLT, EARL IRA................. Maryville ........... General
JARRELL, DONNA KATHLEEN.... Jarrolds Valley,W.Va.. General
JARRELL, ESTHER .............. Jarrolds Valley,W.Va.. Classical
JARRELL, MINNIE AGNES........ Jarrolds Valley,W.Va.. General
KELLER, EARL ROSCOE............ Maryville ........... General
KINNAMON, SAMUEL OSCAR.....:.. Maryville............ Classical
LAMONS, ARTIE ................. Sevierville .......... Classical
LAVASTIDA, ELOISE LOUISE........ Havana, Cuba....... Classical
LAVASTIDA, JULIO ALBERTO......: Havana, Cuba....... Classical
LAWSON, OTHA MERLE........... Maryville ........... General
LAWSON, ROSA ELLEN............ Townsend ........... Classical
LILLARD, HORACE RAY........... Maryville, R. D. 1... Classical
LINDSAY, EDWIN CAMP.......... Alcoa .............. General
LUNSFORD, GORDON ............. Nashville ........... Classical
McCAMMON, OLIVER ............ Maryville ........... General
McCAMPBELL, MILDRED ......... Maryville .:........ Classical
McCONNELL, BERNICE ANNETTE.. Kingsport .......... Classical
McCORMICK, DILLARD HASKELL... Rickman, R. D. 1.... General
McCULLOCH, ORA ELIZABETH..... Mint .............. General
McGRATH, RUTH JUANITA....... Maryville ........... Classical
McKENZIE, HARRY GAINES....... Madisonville ....... General
McLAUGHLIN, CECIL RAY........ Erwin .............. Classical
McMURRAY, KITTIE ............. Chilhowee .......... General
McNEILLY, BEULAH ............. Walland ............ General
McNUTT, HUGH TEDFORD........ Maryville ........... General
McNUTT, ROSS ANDERSON....... Maryville ........... Classical
MAGILL, ROBERT NATHAN........ Madisonville ....... General
MANN, ARTHUR MASON.......... Farm School, N. C.. Classical
MAPLES, HATTIE MAE........... Sevierville ..:...... Classical
MITCHELL, WALTER BURTON...... Rutledge ........... Classical
MONTOTO, CARMINA ............. Havana, Cuba....... Classical
MOOK, JOHN WILLIAM........... Maryville ........... Classical
MOORE, WILLIAM ALEXANDER..... Mosheim ........... General
MOSS, WILLIAM LENOX.......... Silver Point......... Classical

MURRAY, WALTER ALEXANDER.... Greenback .......... Classical
NEVES, HESTER RUTH............ Campobello, S. C.... Classical
NICELY, GOLDIE BEATRICE........ Washburn .......... Classical
NORTON, ANNA BELLE............ Seymour ........... General
NUCHOLS, KATE JANE............ Maryville, R. D. 5... General
OLDHAM, WALTER INDEPENDENCE... Alcoa .............. Classical
ORR, WILLIE ALEXANDER......... Louisville .......... Classical
PAGE, STEVE NATHANIEL......... Hurricane Mills..... General
PARKER, HERMAN MUNK......... Knoxville, R. D. 5... General
PICKEL, ANNA LEE.............. Knoxville, R. D. 11.. General
PICKLE, SAM VERGIL............. Knoxville, R. D. 11.. General
POLK, WILLIAM SAMUEL......... Maryville .......... Classical
PONJUAN, JUAN JOSE............ Havana, Cuba....... General
PRATHER, FRANK ALLEN SOPER... Maryville .......... Classical
PRATT, VERNE LAMAR............ Red Oak, Tex....... General
PUIG, RAMON ................... Havana, Cuba....... General
REAGAN, RUTH ................. Maryville .......... Classical
RICE, VERNON WILSON........... Harlan, Ky.......... Classical
RICKS, GLADYS GERTRUDE........ China Grove, N. C.. Classical
RIDGWAY, MARY VIRGINIA........ Palatka, Fla........ Classical
ROBBINS, GEORGIA McNABB....... Chilhowee .......... General
ROBBINS, JOHN CARL............ Erwin .............. General
ROGERS, LOLA HELEN............ Jellico ............. General
ROWLETT, ROBERT DONNELL....... Medina ............. General
RUBLE, FOX GREER.............. Del Rio ............ General
RUTHERFORD, BERTHA LENORA.... Montcoal, W. Va.... Classical
RYBURN, FRANK LINDSLEY....... Erwin .............. Classical
SANCHEZ, EDUARDO.............. Havana, Cuba....... General
SANDERS, HAZEL ................ Jonesboro, R. D. 10.. Classical
SANDERS, VASHTI ALICE.......... Jonesboro, R. D. 10.. Classical
SANDERS, WILLIE GRAVES........ Jonesboro, R. D. 10.. General
SCOTT, FLOYD CHARLES........... Concord, R. D. 4.... Classical
SEATON, CHARLES INMAN........ Sevierville .......... General
SHAFFER, TOM AMES............. Pittsburgh, Pa....... Classical
SIMPSON, ROBERT L............. Philadelphia ........ General
SMITH, ERNEST ................. Maryville .......... General
SMITH, ROBERT JOHNSON........ Elizabethton ....... General
SMITH, WALTER ................. Hartford ........... General
SMITH, WILBUR ................. Hartford ........... Classical
SNODGRASS, FRANK EDWARD...... Salt Lake City, Utah. General
SPECK, DAVID MAURICE.......... Monterey .......... Classical
SPICKARD, ANDREW WALTER...... Nashville .......... Classical
SPRINKLE, ERNEST DEWIE........ Sweetwater ........ General
STILES, CLIFFORD ALLEN......... DeLand, Fla........ Classical
STRONG, NAOMI BELLE........... Montcoal, W. Va.... General

SWIFT, MARY DIMPLES..........Greenbrier ..........General
TEFFERTELLER, JAMES McNUTT...Maryville, R. D. 2...General
TEFFERTELLER, JOHN STERLING....Maryville, R. D. 3...General
TEMPLEMAN, ELIZABETH MORGAN Alcoa .............Classical
TEMPLIN, WILBUR LESTON........Sevierville, R. D. 10..Classical
THOMAS, PAUL LEGARD..........Cortner ..........Classical
TIPTON, JENNIE ...............Seymour ..........General
TIPTON, JONNIE ...............Townsend ..........General
TIPTON, WILLIE MYRTLE.........Seymour ..........General
TOOLE, MAX GAMBLE............Concord, R. D. 4....Classical
WALDEN, WALTER ..............Jellico, R. D. 2......General
WALLACE, CLYDE DEARMOND.....Maryville ..........General
WALLACE, HELEN ..............Maryville, R. D. 6...General
WATERS, MARGARET LUCILE.......Maryville ..........General
WATTS, JOHN WILLIAM..........Etowah ..........Classical
WELLS, MINNIE GEORGIA.........Mint, R. D. 1........Classical
WESTBROOK, LENA BYRON........Meridian, Miss......Classical
WHETSELL, JESSIE MAE..........Maryville ..........General
WHETSELL, MARTHA NELL........Maryville ..........General
WHITEHEAD, CARSON ...........Rasar .............General
WHITEHEAD, STELLA MAE........Rasar .............General
WILLHITE, CLAUDE THOMAS......Hurricane Mills.....General
WILLIAMS, JAY................Sevierville ..........Classical
WILSON, MARIE ...............Ashland, Ala........Classical
YANG, CHOONG HUYNG..........Seoul, Korea........Classical

## PREPARATORY SPECIAL STUDENTS

ANDERSON, GENEVA.............Maryville, R. D. 4....Music
ATKINS, ANNARINE .............Maryville ..........Expression
BREWER, MARY ................Walland ............General
BURCHFIELD, VIRGINIA DARE......Pineville, Ky........Home Economics
CATLETT, JONNIE WILLIE.........Maryville ..........Music
CLARK, LILLIAN MARIE..........Maryville ..........Music
CLARK, THELMA IRENE..........Townsend ..........Music
COULTER, HASSIE ETTA..........Maryville ..........Home Economics
COULTER, HELEN HENRIETTA......Maryville ..........Art
COWAN, KATE MARY............Maryville ..........Art
CUNNINGHAM, MAC HUNT.......Maryville ..........Expression
DOUGHERTY, EDWARD WILLIE.....Maryville, R. D. 3...Art
EVERETT, VIVIAN VAUGHAN ......Maryville ..........Expression
FRANKLIN, KATHERINE LEE.......Maryville ..........Expression
FRENCH, HELEN MARGARET.......Maryville ..........Music
FRENCH, VAUGHTIE McREYNOLDS. Maryville ..........General
FROW, ALBERTA MAUD...........Maryville ..........Expression

HITCH, NOLA ................... Maryville, R. D. 4... Home Economics
HOLMES, MAY BUCHANAN....... Birmingham, Ala.... Music
HOWARD, KENNETH HOUSTON .... Maryville .......... Music
LANNING, MARTHA ELIZABETH ... Maryville .......... Art
MAGILL, EMMA ................ Maryville .......... Home Economics
MAXWELL, LYDIA LIPSCOMB....... Maryville .......... Music
MOORE, ALURA ................ Chattanooga ........ General
PARKINS, EDNA IRENE.......... Maryville .......... Music
REED, NELLIE EDITH ........... Maryville .......... Music
ROYLSTON, IDA BYRL........... Maryville .......... Music
SMITH, EDWARD DANIEL ........ Maryville, R. D. 8... General
THOMPSON, IDA MAE........... Maryville .......... Home Economics
VEAL, ERNEST PASCAL.......... Bear Creek, Ala.... General
WALKER, BEATRICE GENEVIEVE.... Maryville, R. D. 1... Music
WALKER, HAZEL BLANCHE....... Maryville .......... Expression
WALKER, MINNIE ESTELLE........ Maryville .......... Art
WEBB, SARA MYRTLE........... Sevierville .......... General
WEBSTER, LEE ANNA LUCILE...... Maryville .......... Art
WEST, BERNICE RUTH........... Maryville, R. D. 4... Music
WHITE, ALICE MABEL........... Baylis, Ill.......... General
WILLIS, MARGARET EURETHA..... Rogersville ........ Home Economics
YEAROUT, CORA RANKIN......... Maryville, R. D. 2... Home Economics
YEAROUT, ELSIE LEE............ Maryville .......... Music

# SUMMARY OF ENROLLMENT

## CLASSIFICATION BY DEPARTMENTS

College Department ............................................. 298
Preparatory Department .. .................................... 450

Total.................................................... 748

## CLASSIFICATION BY STATES

| | | | |
|---|--:|---|--:|
| Alabama | 28 | Oklahoma | 3 |
| California | 1 | Pennsylvania | 9 |
| Connecticut | 1 | Rhode Island | 1 |
| Florida | 11 | South Carolina | 6 |
| Georgia | 17 | Tennessee | 480 |
| Illinois | 8 | Texas | 9 |
| Indiana | 11 | Utah | 3 |
| Kentucky | 30 | Virginia | 8 |
| Maryland | 2 | West Virginia | 18 |
| Michigan | 4 | China | 1 |
| Mississippi | 9 | Cuba | 11 |
| Missouri | 5 | England | 1 |
| New Jersey | 8 | Japan | 1 |
| New Mexico | 1 | Korea | 1 |
| New York | 9 | Persia | 1 |
| North Carolina | 29 | Scotland | 1 |
| Ohio | 19 | Syria | 1 |

Total number of students................................. 748

Total number of States and countries..................... 34

# CALENDAR FOR 1918-1919

1918

Sept. 10, Tuesday, 8:00 a. m.-4:00 p. m.—Registration for the fall term.

Sept. 11, Wednesday, 8:45 a. m.—Opening chapel service.

Sept. 11, Wednesday, 9:15 a. m.-3:00 p. m.—Organization of classes.

Sept. 14, Saturday, 2:30 p. m.—Faculty reception.

Sept. 14, Saturday, 8:00 p. m.—Y. M. C. A. and Y. W. C. A. receptions.

Oct. 31, Thursday,—Class social functions.

Nov. 28, Thursday,—Thanksgiving.

Dec. 2, Monday, 8:00 p. m.—Athenian Midwinter.

Dec. 9, Monday, 8:00 p. m.—Alpha Sigma Midwinter.

Dec. 17, 18, 19, Tuesday-Thursday,—Examinations.

Dec. 19, Thursday,—Fall term ends.

1919

Jan. 2, Thursday, 8:00 a. m.-4:00 p. m.—Registration for the winter term.

Jan. 3, Friday, 8:45 a. m.—Opening chapel service,

Jan. 3, Friday, 9:15 a. m.-3:00 p. m.—Organization of classes.

Jan. 4, Saturday, 8:00 p. m.—General college social.

Jan. 20, Monday, 8:00 p. m.—Bainonian Midwinter.

Jan. 27, Monday, 8:00 p. m.—Theta Epsilon Midwinter.

Feb. 2, Sabbath, 7:00 p. m.—February Meetings begin.

Feb. 5, Wednesday, 8:30 a. m.—Meeting of the Directors.

Mar. 15, 18, 19, Saturday, Tuesday, and Wednesday,—Examinations.

Mar. 19, Wednesday,—Winter term ends.

Mar. 20, Thursday, 8:00 a. m.-4:00 p. m.—Registration for the spring term.

Mar. 21, Friday, 8:10 a. m.-3:00 p. m.—Chapel service and regular classes.

May 30, Friday, 8:00 p. m.—Graduation exercises of the Expression Department.

May 31, Saturday,—Examinations begin.

May 31, Saturday, 8:00 p. m.—Graduation exercises of the Music Department.

## JUNE 1-5, SABBATH-THURSDAY,—CENTENNIAL CELEBRATION

June 1, Sabbath, 10:30 a. m.—Baccalaureate sermon.

June 1, Sabbath, 5:40 p. m.—Annual address to the Y. M. C. A. and Y. W. C. A.

June 2, Monday, 8:00 p. m.—Graduation exercises of the Preparatory Department.

June 3, 4, Tuesday, Wednesday,—Examinations.

June 3, Tuesday, 3:00 p. m.—Graduation exercises and exhibit of the Home Economics Department.

June 4, Wednesday, 7:30 p. m.—Senior class play.

**June 5, Thursday,—Commencement and Centennial Celebration.**

# INDEX

# Maryville College
## === Bulletin ===

Vol. XVIII    MAY, 1919    No. 1

## CONTENTS
PAGE

Published four times a year by

### MARYVILLE COLLEGE
**Maryville, Tennessee**

Entered May 24, 1904, at Maryville, Tenn., as second-class
matter. Acceptance for mailing at special rate of
postage provided for in Section 1103, Act of October
3, 1917, authorized February 10, 1919.